FRANCES PERKINS
FIRST WOMAN CABINET MEMBER

FRANCES PERKINS
FIRST WOMAN CABINET MEMBER

Emily Keller

MORGAN REYNOLDS

PUBLISHING

Greensboro, North Carolina

20th Century
Leaders

Dwight D. Eisenhower

Lyndon Baines Johnson

Thurgood Marshall

Ronald Reagan

Marcus Garvey

Richard Nixon

Jimmy Carter

Madeleine Albright

Frances Perkins

FRANCES PERKINS: FIRST WOMAN CABINET MEMBER

Copyright © 2006 by Emily Keller

Library of Congress Cataloging-in-Publication Data

Keller, Emily.
    Frances Perkins : first woman cabinet member / Emily Keller.
        p. cm.
    Includes bibliographical references and index.
    ISBN-13: 978-1-931798-91-4 (library binding)
    ISBN-10: 1-931798-91-5 (library binding)
    1. Perkins, Frances, 1880-1965. 2. United States. Dept. of Labor--Biography-
-Juvenile literature. 3. Women cabinet officers--United States--Biography--Juve-
nile literature. 4. Women social reformers--United States--Biography--Juvenile
literature. I. Title.
    HD8073.P38K44 2006
    331.092--dc22
    [B]
                                                    2006023971

Printed in the United States of America
First Edition

To my daughters,
Tammyanne and Barbie Jean
These are my jewels

CONTENTS

Frances Perkins. (Library of Congress)

ONE

Happy Days

It was around eight o'clock in the evening on February 22, 1932, when Frances Perkins presented herself at the house on 65th Street in New York City. Perkins, an unassuming, middle-aged lady, simply but fashionably dressed, entered the once elegant entrance hall that now had its oriental rug rolled up and set aside. The chairs, tables and even the ash-strewn floor were littered with newspapers, coats, hats, briefcases, and overshoes.

Her host, New York Governor Franklin Roosevelt, had just been elected the thirty-second president of the United States. Perkins was guided to the president-elect's study on the second floor. The big, handsome man greeted her from his wheelchair in his familiar, jovial manner. Roosevelt, who had been afflicted with polio as a young man, could not stand for long periods. Roosevelt and Perkins had worked together in New York politics for years. Most recently she had served as his New York industrial commissioner and had helped him deal with the Great Depression, the economic crisis that had gripped their state, and the nation, for the past three years. Roosevelt had earned his national reputation with his efforts to alleviate the worst aspects of the depression in New York and was now faced with the same problems, but on a national scale.

At this meeting Roosevelt introduced her to Harold Ickes, a stocky, blond lawyer from the Midwest, who was to become secretary of the interior. Once Ickes left the room, Roosevelt cut to the chase: "I've been thinking things over and I've decided I want you to be secretary of labor," he said.

Perkins thanked him for the honor of offering to make her the first female federal cabinet member in U.S. history. Then she asked whether he should not appoint an official from a labor union instead. Roosevelt replied, "The time has come for all working people, organized and unorganized, to have more political consideration." He wanted to accomplish for the nation's workers what had been done for those in New York State, and he wanted her help.

Perkins replied that if she accepted the position of secretary of labor, she would want to go the extra mile to get a great deal done. She outlined an ambitious program of labor legislation and economic improvement that she thought Roosevelt might consider too ambitious.

First on her agenda was federal aid to states for unemployment relief and public works projects to put people back to work. She wanted to improve the lives of those who still had jobs by abolishing child labor, establishing laws on maximum hours worked per day and week, and on minimum wages. She also wanted to create a federal employment service. Her pet project was a national workers' compensation system to aid those who were injured on the job.

Roosevelt agreed with her that much needed to be done. After their hourlong conversation, Perkins agreed to become secretary of labor. She was about to enter the most dynamic and revolutionary presidency of the twentieth century. The work she and the president would do would permanently alter the way people worked and lived in the United States.

Perkins had been preparing for this important job most of her life. She had been named Fanny Coralie Perkins when she was born to Frederick W. and Susan E. (Wight) Bean, in Boston, Massachusetts, on April 10, 1880. She was named Fanny after her mother's older sister.

Fanny Perkins grew up in Worcester, Massachusetts. Her closest friend growing up was her cousin Nan. The girls spent the summers with their widowed grandmother, Cynthia Otis Perkins, at the family farm in Newcastle, Maine. The farm had a large brick house, a wooden carriage house, a red barn, a privy, an icehouse, and a chicken coop. Maple trees, lilac and barberry bushes encircled the homestead. Behind the house a lane descended through woods of oak and pine, through a meadow and down to the shores of the Damariscotta River, where the family kept a canoe with a rowboat and a sailboat.

Fanny Perkins at age four. (Courtesy of Mount Holyoke Archives and Special Collections.)

Her mother, Susan Perkins, ran a hospitable home in Worcester. She had the help of a maid, a cook, and a nurse for Fanny. Susan Perkins was fun and outgoing. She could sketch and draw and delighted the children by making clay animal figures. She also sewed and tried to teach the girls. Perkins later described her mother as a late sleeper who allowed Perkins' grandmother to run the household after she came to live with them. Susan Perkins, although emotional and unconventional at times, was a generous woman who helped take care of children when an aunt or cousin fell ill, and helped needy families. At times, the Perkins family even helped others with their rent.

Fred Perkins was more reserved than his wife. He was an amateur scholar who loved to read Greek poetry. He began teaching Fanny Greek grammar when she was eight.

The Perkinses were active members of the Plymouth Congregational Church. They devoted time to charity work and took pride in their country and ancestors, particularly James Otis, a fiery Revolutionary War patriot, and his sister, Mercy Otis Warren. When she was ten, Fanny's parents presented her with a tricorn, or three-cornered hat, such as American revolutionaries wore. She loved the hat and wore it often.

Fred Perkins ran a profitable retail and wholesale stationery business and circulating library. As Fanny grew up, her tastes and interests were more like her father's than her mother's or her sister Ethel's, who was four years younger. Fanny was plump and had an oval face with olive complexion and expressive, dark eyes. She liked to read and to argue. Sometimes she babbled, and her father would admonish her, "If you have anything to say, say it definitely and stop." Fanny was usually serious and thoughtful, original and creative. However, she was also very shy and had few friends except for Nan.

The Oxford Street Grammar School, a small private school, offered a class for sacred study in which Fanny read the gospels and examined them for personal meaning. From the Oxford Street Grammar School, Fanny entered Worcester Classical High School, where she learned Latin and Greek. Most of the students were boys. Fanny was only an average student but a star debater. The principal, Edward Goodwin, encouraged his pupils to go on to institutions of higher learning. Fanny's mother believed a suitable marriage might be the next step in her daughter's life and had lined up various suitors, but her father thought Fanny might make a good teacher. She applied to Mount Holyoke College in 1897.

When she entered Mount Holyoke in South Hadley, Massachusetts, at the age of eighteen, Fanny found outstanding teachers who inspired her to work hard and to be

Mary Lyon, chemist and pioneering educator, founded Mount Holyoke in 1837. When Fanny attended the school sixty years later, the college remained faithful to its founder's dream of providing female scholars with an education that rivaled the all-male Ivy League schools in quality. (Courtesy of Mount Holyoke College Archives and Special Collections.)

exact in her studies. She took a required chemistry course in her sophomore year and had to struggle to pass, but stayed with it out of a fierce intellectual pride. She even adopted chemistry as her major, with physics and biology as a minor. It was unusual for a girl to major in a science, but Fanny welcomed the mental discipline.

The years at Mount Holyoke were happy for Perkins. The campus was beautiful; the grounds sloped gently to a stream and pond with an old stone mill. Dams created upper and lower lakes with shores banked by woods. Perkins's marks at college were not always good, but she took the hardest courses and passed them. This gave her confidence, and, she thought, built her character. In her junior year she was elected class vice-president.

In her senior year she was elected class president. Perkins was a nonconformist who sometimes broke rules—such as "lights out"—when she wanted to talk. This may have annoyed the school administration, but she was good-natured and popular with the girls, who called her "Perk" or "Perky." A few students agreed with her father that she talked too much and labeled her the "loquacious linguist."

Perkins appeared in many plays and briefly thought of being a writer or an actress. She was limited in her college activities, however, because of her difficult science and math classes. Still, despite the demands of that "wretched physics laboratory," she was voted "the Girl who had done most for the Class" and elected permanent class president. She was also chairwoman of the YWCA committee.

Frances Perkins heads the Mount Holyoke graduating class of 1902 (left). (Courtesy of Mount Holyoke College Archives and Special Collections.)

Perkins fit right in to the school's stringent religious atmosphere and prayer meetings. Religion appealed to her, particularly the ideas that vanity was sin and good works and charity were to be practiced. In contrast, the poet Emily Dickinson, who enrolled in 1847, did well in her work but found Mount Holyoke's rules to be tedious and the constant stress on sin and duty wearying. Dickinson withdrew at the end of her first year.

In addition to hard work, there was also plenty of fun and frivolity at the school, including lawn tennis and kite-flying. In winter, Perkins was an active skater and organized horse-drawn sleighing parties. Perkins, who stood five-foot-five and usually wore her hair in a bun, made friends at Mount Holyoke that lasted a lifetime.

One of her teachers, American History Professor Annah May Soule, took her students into paper and textile mills in Massachusetts and Connecticut and asked them to make a survey of working conditions. They discovered that one serious accident, such as the loss of a man's hand, could drive a steady, working family into poverty. At that time there was no workers' compensation, unemployment insurance, minimum wage, or maximum hours. Many employees were immigrants who could scarcely speak English, much less negotiate for better pay and working conditions. The burden of accidents, which grew increasingly common as new and dangerous machinery was developed, fell on the worker and his family. Many employees worked a twelve-hour day, six or seven days a week.

Factory work was also unsteady. Layoffs could happen with little warning. Fanny had been brought up in a family that, although committed to doing "good works," had ascribed to the typical middle-class ideas of the time. One of these ideas was that the vast majority of poverty was caused by excessive drinking or laziness, poor financial management, or a lack of moral values. For the first time she saw that poverty was more likely due to severe injury caused by a lack of safety devices on machines, or by irregular employment created by the business cycle and the absence of a social "safety net" to help workers through bad times.

Around this time Perkins read Jacob Riis's study of the tenements in New York, *How the Other Half Lives*. She became committed to Riis's philosophy of bringing justice to those in poverty. The book, which came with statistics, vivid descriptions and shocking photos, made such an impression on her that she spoke about it with her parents.

That same year, on February 20, Perkins heard Florence Kelley speak at Mount Holyoke. Kelley, a dynamic social reformer, advocated for the prohibition of child labor and for limiting the number of hours that women could be forced to work. Kelley had served four years as chief inspector of factories for Governor John P. Altgeld of Illinois, had

Florence Kelley, as she appeared several years later in her career as a factory inspector and regulation reformer. (Library of Congress)

worked with Jane Addams, a prominent social reformer, at Hull House in Chicago, and had gone to New York in 1899 to enlarge the local Consumers League into a national movement. She was a large woman with heavy braids of dark hair crowning her head. Dressed always in black, she was a crusader and a gifted speaker.

Kelley used her maiden name, although she had been married and had three children. After graduating from Cornell University, she had been refused entrance into the law school at the University of Pennsylvania because of her sex. She then went on a walking tour of English industrial counties, where she was shocked by the exploitation of workers in the factories that had sprung up and the urban poverty and misery. The trip determined her life's work.

After the speech Perkins met Kelley, who spoke movingly of the poverty and misery she had seen in her work. She had told the audience about watching a boy being abused at a glass factory in Illinois, which was only one of thousands of incidences that happened every day. Attending Kelley's speech was one of the most critical events in Perkins's life. She said later that it helped her realize the need for the role she would take within the federal government. Her life's work had been determined.

TWO

The Pursuit of
Social Justice

After Perkins graduated from Mount Holyoke in June 1902, she returned home for a year of social activities, parties, and dating. During that time she received one job offer as an analytical chemist in a canning factory. Her parents regarded this as unseemly employment for a proper young lady. They wanted her to teach until she married. Perkins, adrift, worked as a substitute teacher and spent one summer in New York unsuccessfully looking for work as an actress.

While in Worcester, Perkins taught Sunday school and participated in church activities. She organized a club for teen-aged girls who worked in stores and at a candy factory for low wages. She based the club on what she had read about Hull House, the settlement house in Chicago run by Jane Addams. The underlying idea of a settlement house was that men and women who had recently graduated from college would make a "settlement" in a poor area, sharing the problems of the residents and working with them to reform neighborhood conditions. The emphasis was on education, culture, and improvement projects, such as building and maintaining parks, playgrounds, housing, and sanitation. The settlement houses also contained political clubs. For example, Hull House offered the Jane Club, a place for girls to go to demand improvement in working conditions. Settlement houses were open to persons of all races, creeds, and nationalities and usually contained kindergartens, nurseries, and clubs for boys and girls. They also fed the poor.

The girls in the club Perkins organized in Worcester had exercises and games in the gym, entertaining excursions, and educational classes. When one of the girls had her hand cut off in a candy dipper, the factory simply sent her home. Perkins arranged for a doctor to treat her and tried unsuccessfully to collect money from the employer. In the end, a clergyman intervened and persuaded the manufacturer to give the girl one hundred dollars.

In 1904 Perkins accepted a teaching position at Ferry Hall, an exclusive school in Lake Forest, Illinois. There she taught physics and biology and wrote short stories in her free time.

That same year, Theodore Roosevelt was elected president of the United States. He had first come to office in 1901, after the assassination of President William McKinley. His inaugural address in March 1905 further persuaded Perkins that "the pursuit of social justice" was a noble vocation. She later explained, "he had been the first to reach the peak of political life who pointed out a social obligation: the sufferings of the poor, of the oppressed, of the immigrants, and the right and duty of those with advantages to do something about it."

Theodore Roosevelt was the first president to advocate some of the positions taken by the reform, or progressive, movement that urged social improvement by government action. Roosevelt left office in 1909, but in 1912 he ran again as the candidate of the Progressive Party, which was nicknamed the Bull Moose Party.

Progressivism's roots stretched back to the 1880s. It began as a largely agrarian movement aimed at more government control of corporations, the abolition of corporate trusts and monopolies, and the limiting of corporate dominance of government. Progressivism marked an entire generation of idealistic young Americans. People such as Jane Addams, Franklin Roosevelt and Perkins became convinced of the necessity for a strong national government to create a barrier between the demands of industrial capitalism and the needs of society and the fair treatment of workers. As she later noted, "Out of the period that I was in school a whole generation, particularly women emerged, but men, too, who had a great passion for social justice."

While teaching at Ferry Hall, Perkins spent her weekends and vacations volunteering at Hull House and another settlement house in Chicago. She came to know Jane Addams, who told her that settlement houses had a

Jane Addams founded the U.S. settlement house movement. She became the first American woman to win a Nobel Peace Prize and was a tireless reformer for working people, African Americans, and women. (Library of Congress)

dual purpose. One was to help the people in the neighborhood. The other, larger purpose was to make others aware of what was needed in distressed neighborhoods. Addams believed that this awareness would help to prompt municipalities to improve those neighborhoods.

Settlement work appealed to Perkins because she was searching for a vocation with a purpose. During this time she changed her name from Fannie to Frances. She also told her family she was considering converting to Catholicism. When this upset them, she compromised by becoming an Episcopalian, "half-way to the Catholics," she remarked later. She was drawn to the Catholic and Episcopal faiths by their rituals. She remarked once that transfers of power would be accomplished more surely and with less bitterness if each party knew in advance where to stand, what words to say, and which gestures to make. She liked staged events. She also favored the church's liturgy and the high-church vestments, which pointed out the seasons of the church year. In addition, the Episcopal Church was affiliated with the labor movement. She may also have been attracted by the selflessness, the charity and the love for the poor and unfortunate vividly portrayed in lives of the saints. Perkins remained a devout Episcopalian all her life.

Believing the Democrats were more concerned with the poor, she announced to her staunchly Republican family that she was now a Democrat. Her announcement was more for shock value, as women could not vote.

During the Christmas break in 1905, Perkins went to live at Chicago Commons, another settlement house. Fred Perkins had long denounced trade unions, but Graham Taylor, who founded Chicago Commons, convinced Perkins that trade unions would be the engine of progressivism. He believed that if every working man and woman joined a union, their wages would be sufficient to support them, and families would be able to look after themselves. There would be no need for charity societies and settlements.

When she was twenty-seven, Perkins decided her vocation would be in settlement work, not teaching. She left Ferry Hall in June, 1907. Through a friend, she learned of a position as general secretary for the Philadelphia Research and Protective Association. The Philadelphia Research and Protective Association worked with immigrants and African Americans from the South. As the agency's only employee, Perkins earned fifty dollars a month, less than she had received from teaching. Rather than ask her parents for money, she pawned her watch.

American cities were growing rapidly, expanding upwards and outwards. Manufacturing was booming. Automobile production was the hot new industry. As production

Two settlement houses, Hull House (left) *and Henry Street* (right), *advertise some of the programs offered to the communities they serve.* (Library of Congress)

of autos increased, new roads were built to link small towns to big cities. Thousands of people were lured into the city by the promise of good-paying jobs. But the urban industrial boom had its underside, especially for women, who were sometimes told they would be doing respectable work but when they arrived in cities were forced to work as indentured servants or prostitutes. Perkins arranged for people to meet incoming boats and trains to try to help new arrivals avoid such traps.

Not everyone was pleased with Perkins's work. One rainy night, as she was walking home, two men followed her. She recognized one of the men as a pimp who ran a crooked employment agency. When she walked faster, he sped up. Her father had told her what to do in this type of situation. She hurried around a corner, stopped, hit them with her umbrella, and began to scream the name of the man she knew, "Sam Smith! Sam Smith!" The men fled.

Some good came of this frightening incident. When she reported it to the police and some socially prominent friends, the city closed down several of the worst employment agencies and passed ordinances requiring all lodgings to be licensed. Perkins was careful not to tell her parents about the attempted attack or about living and working in slum areas—she knew they would not approve.

Among her closest friends in Philadelphia were George and Joe Caylor, who were both active in the Socialist Party. Socialists think that many of society's ills come from the disparity of wealth that results from the ownership of private property. Society can never attain true equality as long as individuals or corporations are able to accumulate vast amounts of property and wealth, while others have to struggle for survival by working for the wealthy. This was not a popular position in the United States, and the socialist label was often attached to anyone who worked to better the conditions of workers and the poor. In the late nineteenth and early twentieth centuries socialist ideas did appeal to many of those who despaired at the vast inequities generated by the rapid industrialization of the era. It also appealed to some on a more cultural basis, such as women who thought true sexual equality was not possible under capitalism.

Perkins had for a long time questioned the excesses of capitalism. She finally became convinced that capitalism inherently led to a large, oppressed underclass and she joined the Socialist Party in 1909.

There might have been a more personal reason for joining when she did. George Caylor later said, "From the admiration Perkins had for [my brother] Joe and the fondness with which she spoke of him when we met, I could not help but assume that she would have married him, had he asked her." But Joe Caylor was married to the labor movement. He was an intellectual and, his brother claimed, "actually a confirmed bachelor from his early twenties." While it is not known if Perkins felt a romantic attraction for Joe Caylor, she certainly admired and respected his dedication to and knowledge of labor legislation.

At age twenty-nine Perkins wrote to her classmates that

she now considered herself a spinster. Around the same time, she returned to school and began taking courses in economics at the University of Pennsylvania. With the help of Simon Patten, a professor she admired, she won a $500 fellowship to Columbia University in New York City. She planned to learn how to conduct surveys and other methods of social research. She hoped to earn a master's degree in the new field of sociology. Her ultimate goal remained the same—to work for social justice for the poor. She hoped the education would help her gain practical experience and the theoretical knowledge necessary to better achieve this goal.

After moving, Perkins quickly fell in love with New York City. She enjoyed the artistic and social life and frequented art exhibits, tea dances, and quaint restaurants near her home in Greenwich Village. She first met Franklin Delano Roosevelt, a wealthy, educated, and fiercely ambitious young lawyer, at a tea dance. She only noticed him because he was loudly defending his distant cousin, Theodore Roosevelt, and his progressive ideas.

Although busy with school and social work, Perkins continued to pursue artistic endeavors. Georgia O'Keefe and Diego Rivera, a Mexican artist who specialized in socialist themes, were her favorite artists, but her favorite picture was *Portrait of a Little Girl* by George Bellows. "A child of the poor—no question about it. You know from the look on her face," Perkins said. Perkins liked to sketch and paint and to write short stories. She also wrote faithfully to her classmates and made a remarkable number of

Franklin Delano Roosevelt, in his office, soon after Perkins met him at the tea dance. (Courtesy of the Franklin Delano Roosevelt Library.)

acquaintances for such a shy person. She was always ready for an outing to the beaches at Staten Island. Sometimes she and her friends picnicked or made bonfires, and other times just enjoyed the ferry boat ride.

Her most constant escort was Sinclair "Red" Lewis. The future Nobel Prize-winning author of *Main Street, Babbitt,*

Elmer Gantry, and *Ann Vickers* was still a struggling writer. In his novel *Ann Vickers,* published in 1933, Lewis probably based the main character partly on Perkins. The novel is a story of a modern American woman: a liberal, feminist social worker who only becomes a fully realized woman when she learns to love a man. Vickers even discovers the meaning of feminism through love.

Lewis remained an outsider to many of Perkins' friends. Some of them, particularly the men, regarded him as a nuisance and did not take him seriously. Lewis angered them by ridiculing their theories. He was tall, red-headed, scrawny, and uncoordinated. Perkins thought he had a "peculiar style of ugliness" exaggerated by his cheap, ready-made suits of dark blue. Lewis was also a card-carrying Socialist.

One warm summer evening when all the windows in Perkins's apartment house were open, Lewis proposed marriage to her "at the top of his lungs." Neither took it seriously. He was a mimic and cut-up, and she found him amusing.

The Henry Street Settlement House in New York figured most prominently in her life at this time. There Perkins met people such as the idealistic followers of John Purroy Mitchel, who would soon be the reform mayor of New York. It is likely she also met Paul C. Wilson there, the man she would later marry. He was the brilliant secretary to John Mitchel, and an outstanding financial statistician.

Florence Kelley, Josephine Lowell, and John Graham Brooks first established the National Consumers League in 1899 at the Henry Street Settlement House. It was founded to collect information on stores and factories. Its inspectors reported on safety, sanitation, and working conditions and released the information to the public. They also lobbied for the end of child labor and improved working conditions. Their slogan was "investigate, agitate, legislate."

Perkins joined the League and soon became immersed in investigations. Her dedication to her work won her election to the post of executive secretary in April 1910. She received her master's degree in economics and sociology two months later. Her master's thesis was entitled "A Study of Malnutrition in 107 Children from Public School 51." Public School 51 was located in what was known as Hell's Kitchen, a poor district in New York City.

Perkins wrote a report, later sent to the city's board of health, detailing her investigations into one hundred bakeries in New York. She had discovered people sleeping on bakery floors where they worked sixteen to eighteen hours a day in poorly lit and filthy cellars. Rats were attracted to the stored bags of flour and infested the mostly underground kitchens and storerooms.

As Perkins spent time drumming up reports, she discovered that she was also a skilled orator. She spoke to teachers' conventions about child labor laws. She knew teachers would help. She told them that children were working sixty to seventy-two hours a week in factories full of dust and fumes, which often led to death. She ended her talks with a poem by Sarah Cleghorn:

Students in a school on the lower east side of New York City. The picture was taken by Jacob Riis, whose book about New York's underclass helped push Perkins towards her life's work. (Courtesy of the Granger Collection.)

The golf links lie so near the mill,
That nearly every day,
The laboring children can look out
And see the men at play.

In December 1910 an engineer and two fire prevention experts helped Perkins investigate a factory fire in Newark, New Jersey, in which twenty-five young women were killed. Early in 1911, she compiled data that served as the basis for safety recommendations for textile mills, laundries, and other similar industries that mostly employed women. Perkins shared her knowledge with a journalist, Mary Heaton Vorse, and with influential citizens who she hoped would exert pressure to change the situation.

March 25, 1911, was "a fine, bright spring afternoon," Perkins remembered. It was also a day that would live forever in American labor history. She later described what she saw as a fire consumed the Triangle Shirtwaist Factory and killed almost 150 workers:

> We heard the fire engines and rushed into the Square [Washington Square East] to see what was going on. We saw the smoke pouring out of the building [the Asch building which housed the Triangle Shirtwaist Factory]. We got there just as they started to jump. I shall never forget the frozen horror which came over us as we stood with our hands on our throats watching that horrible sight, knowing that there was no help. They came down in twos and threes, jumping together in a kind of desperate hope. The life nets were broken. The firemen kept shouting for them not to jump. But they had no choice; the flames were right behind them for by this time the fire was far gone.

Firemen on the scene had spread their nets, but they were not sturdy enough to catch the women who, engulfed in flames, hurled themselves out of the eighth and ninth floors. Some hung from windowsills until their fingers gave way. Bodies cracked on the sidewalks; none who fell or jumped survived. Blood splattered on the fire horses whinnying in terror as they strained in their harnesses, trying to escape the flames, the screams and the sounds of bodies slamming the pavement. The carnage lasted almost an hour. Perkins, although sick to her stomach, refused to turn away. She wanted to sear the images in her mind and on her heart as a reminder of why she had to fight to stop such tragedies from happening again. "Out of that terrible episode came a self-examination of stricken conscience, of public guilt, in which the people of this state saw for the first time the individual worth and value of each of those 146 people who fell or were burned in that great fire."

Testimony later revealed that the blaze at the Triangle Shirtwaist Factory was caused by the same type of factory conditions Perkins had witnessed elsewhere. Exit doors had been locked to keep union organizers out and to prevent workers from passing out stolen merchandise. The building was overcrowded, the floors littered with cloth remnants and other flammable debris. The fire alarm system was dilapidated.

On April 2, the Metropolitan Opera House, filled to capacity with 3,500 people, held a memorial service for the dead factory workers. Rose Schneiderman, twenty-nine, was a union organizer who had tried unsuccessfully to unionize the Triangle Factory the year before. The factory had fired all union members. Schneiderman was a garment worker and a leader of the Women's Trade Union League. She spoke quietly but eloquently about the dead girls' bodies, about those maimed for life, about mothers who went insane over the loss of their daughters, and about how cheaply life was treated.

Three days later 120,000 people marched in a cold rain for six hours in a grim funeral procession held by Local 25 of the International Ladies' Garment Workers Union for seven unidentified victims. Nearly 400,000 onlookers gathered to watch. Later, in court, the factory owners were acquitted of all charges. They had obeyed all existing fire safety laws. Out-of-court settlements resulted in an average payment of 75 dollars per dead employee.

After the Triangle Fire, Perkins served on a committee that petitioned Governor John A. Dix for state action to improve the working conditions in factories. Perkins's committee, along with other protest groups, eventually succeeded in pressuring the New York State legislature to create the Factory Investigating Commission, established on June 30, 1911.

THREE

Fiery Young Idealist

On November 14, 1911, Perkins testified before the Factory Investigating Commission as an expert witness on conditions inside the New York City cellar bakeries. She advised and served as an expert witness for the Committee on Safety of the city of New York and was made director of investigations for the Factory Investigating Commission. Robert F. Wagner and Al Smith, majority leaders in the New York State Senate and Assembly, were chairman and vice-chairman of the commission. Mary Drier, president of the National Women's Trade Union League, was also a member. Drier was a young, wealthy civic leader, a passionate reformer, and an able, dedicated leader who had once been arrested for participating in a strike of shirtwaist workers.

Perkins continued her salaried job with the National

Consumers League. Despite her busy schedule, she accepted an invitation to teach sociology at Adelphi College from 1911 to 1912. She also spoke to many organizations about the need for child labor laws and lobbied for legislation in Albany, the state capital. There she worked toward

Perkins, as the director of investigations for the Factory Investigating Commission. (Courtesy of Frances Perkins Papers, Rare Book and Manuscript Library, Columbia University.)

passage of a bill to limit the number of hours women and boys under eighteen could work.

However, the bill faced strong opposition. Perkins sought the help of a powerful politician, state Senator Tim "Big Tim" Sullivan. Big Tim cast his vote for the bill, then left for New York City. Opponents to the bill managed to defeat the bill in his absence. Perkins urged a supporter to have the bill reconsidered and raced to a phone to call Big Tim. Sullivan rushed back with his cousin in a taxi, which stalled on the road. They ran the rest of the way and arrived moments before the doors were locked for the night. Sullivan then persuaded senators to change their votes. It had taken five years, but the fifty-four-hour bill was finally passed in March 1912.

Although Franklin Roosevelt, then a state senator, later claimed he helped get the bill passed, and did vote for it, Perkins was never sure he actually supported it. In her book *The Roosevelt I Knew,* Perkins wrote, "I took it hard that a young man who had so much spirit did not do so well in this." Louis Howe, Roosevelt's advisor, claimed that Roosevelt filibustered the senate with a lecture on birds while they waited for Sullivan to return. Perkins heard no such lecture. The bill was antagonistic to the interests of Dutchess County farmers, Roosevelt's constituents. Many of the farmers employed women and children to harvest and can produce, prompting Roosevelt's lukewarm support of the bill.

New York state politics would turn out to be an excellent training ground for both Perkins and Roosevelt. Much of what happened in the legislature and assembly was controlled by political machines and factions. The largest player in the Democratic Party was Tammany Hall, centered in New York City. Tammany Hall, an urban New York City-based political machine, controlled the Democratic Party in that area. It had started out catering to Irish and other immigrants in the city and won support by controlling patronage, or government jobs, and by seeing that constituents received service, but it had long been corrupt by the early twentieth century. Many in its leadership had grown wealthy from making deals with business owners and others, and Perkins and Roosevelt, who were part of the small group of reformers in the party, saw Tammany as their enemy.

In May 1912, Perkins went to work as executive secretary for the Committee on Safety, a paid position. She continued to be called as a witness for various committees about fire, accidents, and sanitation. A fiery young idealist, Perkins was a memorable character—an attractive woman in an ankle-length raglan-shouldered greatcoat and billowy plumed tricorn hat.

Perkins led Factory Investigating Commission members on factory tours throughout New York State. Al Smith, a member who grew up poor and mostly uneducated in New York City's East Side, would later become governor of New York. Smith was a member of Tammany but held a genuine interest in reform and was sometimes able to convince Charles Murphy, the Tammany boss, to support reforms that affected his constituents. Smith taught Perkins about lobbying when he was an assemblyman and she first came to Albany. Another member of the commission was a portly state senator named Robert Wagner. In Auburn, the group saw women climbing down a rope ladder after a ten-hour shift in a factory. Perkins made sure that the heavyset Wagner crawled through a tiny hole in the factory wall so he could see for himself the iron ladder that the owners said was a fire escape. The so-called fire escape ended twelve feet off the ground.

Like many reformers, Perkins also took up the fight for women's suffrage. She spoke for the cause in public and quickly learned the value of telling the crowd a funny story. She realized that if the crowd laughed with her, they sided with her and not the men who heckled and jeered.

In June 1912 Perkins went to the Democratic National Convention in Baltimore, where Woodrow Wilson won the nomination. She traveled with two friends, Henry Bruere and Paul C. Wilson, economists interested in government. Unbeknownst to their friends, Wilson and Perkins had fallen in love.

In the spring of 1913, Perkins traveled to England. Reluctant to marry, she wanted to appraise the direction of her life. She traveled through factory towns and, instead of the usual tourist occupations, examined the poverty and industrial areas.

While vacationing in Maine the following August at her grandmother's house, she wrote Wilson every day, sometimes twice a day. She composed eight-page letters about the ache of loneliness and about the joys before them. She could hardly bear the separation. Wilson replied, "I feel you and

Paul C. Wilson. (From *Madame Secretary, Frances Perkins* by George Martin.)

your perfect love have power to make me see things anew. . . . I adore and worship you, beloved, dearly beloved."

One month later, on September 26, 1913, they were married at Grace Episcopal Church in New York. No family or friends were present. Both were reserved in nature and had concealed their wedding plans. She was thirty-three, he thirty-seven. Wilson was handsome, of middle height, with thick, dark hair and square-jawed features. He was also quiet, well-mannered, and unaggressive. Perkins dressed herself and walked to the church. Strangers were their witnesses.

Wilson, from a wealthy family, had graduated from Dartmouth College and the University of Chicago. The new mayor had appointed him his assistant secretary. Perkins and Wilson agreed their political activities would be kept separate.

In addition to their salaries, Wilson had money of his own. He and Perkins rented a small house and hired help. Perkins decorated the house with fine colonial furniture. They also rented what she called a "shack in the country" on Long Island, where they could swim and take walks in the woods. Their neighbors, Henry Bruere, Robert Moses, and their wives and children, were their close friends. Robert Moses, an avid swimmer, worked as a research associate with Paul Wilson. He would later become the New York City planner and transform the city and state by building highways, public parks, beaches and bridges.

Not everyone was pleased about Perkins's marriage. In 1913, social workers and teachers were not expected to marry. It was assumed they would devote all their time and energy to their professions. One friend even lamented, "Oh, Frances, why did you marry? Oh dear, you were such a promising person. Why did you marry?"

Although private and reticent, the couple was very much in love. Perkins planned to have children, and as her paid job for the Committee on Safety came to an end, she decided to replace it with volunteer work. She did not want to assume her husband's name, but had a difficult time keeping her maiden name. When registering in hotels, she had to sign in as Mrs. Wilson, which was how her mother always introduced her.

In the spring of 1915 Perkins gave birth to a child who

died shortly afterwards. She kept her feelings and thoughts about this tragedy to herself. As a result of the pregnancy, she contracted septicemia, or blood poisoning, and was forced to spend several months in bed. Fellow lobbyists from the Consumers League, such as Pauline Goldmark, kept her up to date on bills before the legislature.

On surprise visits to many factories, usually at dawn, the Factory Investigating Commission had seen five, six, and seven-year-olds snapping beans and shelling peas beside their mothers. They also saw unsafe machinery. In 1915 Perkins wrote the commission's final report. Thirty-six new

Children working at a vegetable cannery in 1912. (Courtesy of the Granger Collection.)

laws were passed in New York, making it a national leader in improving sanitation, safety, and working conditions in factories. However, Perkins constantly worried that the New York State legislature, controlled by business interests, would repeal the laws she had worked so hard to pass. The commission's report also brought about a complete reorganization of the old state labor department and the creation of a new industrial commission to supplement it.

Early the following year, Perkins's father passed away. Perkins became pregnant again soon thereafter and had a healthy baby girl in December. She named the baby Susanna Winslow Perkins Wilson, after an ancestor who was the wife of the second governor of the Plymouth Colony.

In 1917, Perkins became executive director of the New York Council of Organizations for War Service. She coordinated various groups and agencies, honing her talents as an administrator. That same year, the United States entered World War I, and New York women won the right to vote.

Soon after, a group of nine women, including Perkins, founded the Maternity Center Association, a national volunteer group in existence today. Perkins, who understood the trauma of losing a child and becoming ill from complications after birth, was executive secretary. The organization's purpose was to combat the high death rates of mothers and babies in the months before and after birth. Perkins called it "the most successful piece of social work I have ever seen organized." She created the administrative structure of the association. Her position

Frances Perkins sits for a formal portrait with her five month old daughter Susanna. (Courtesy of Mount Holyoke Archives and Special Collections.)

was voluntary and unsalaried, with flexible hours and a simple routine for an experienced administrator.

As Perkins spent time with the Maternity Center Association, her husband became ill. He suffered from a mental illness that caused him to experience sudden bouts of excitement and depression—most likely what is today known as bipolar disorder. He often drank to excess as a form of self-medication. He sometimes had to be hospitalized or at least have an attendant, euphemistically called a "secretary," on hand. Wilson worked intermittently until early in 1929. His last job was with an insurance company.

Just as Perkins was winding down her hours at work so she could spend more time at home with her daughter, her husband lost all their money gambling in gold stocks. The careless gambling was another symptom of his illness. Perkins realized she would have to take responsibility for the family's finances. In an effort to save money, they moved to an apartment with enough rooms to allow her mother to come for long visits in the winter, entertained less, and relied on part-time help. Mental illness was not always well understood and could often isolate its victims.

That same year, Al Smith ran for governor of New York. His Catholicism and his stance against the prohibition of alcohol hurt him upstate and in rural areas. Still, he had the support of Tammany Hall in New York City, which put him over the top. Although Tammany Hall was notorious as a group of powerful, corruption-tinged politicians, Smith was known for his honesty.

In January, Smith summoned Perkins to Albany. "How would you like to be a member of the Industrial Commission of the State of New York?" he asked her. The Industrial Commission was created to follow up on the laws and regulations that had been passed to improve working conditions in New York factories and other businesses. Smith had campaigned on the issue of reforming the Commission to make it more effective. He thought Perkins would be a strong ally to have as he began his reforms.

The idea was startling to Perkins. No woman in New

York had ever been appointed to anything but an advisory board. Smith explained his decision:

> I think the Industrial Commission is in terrible condition. We brought that out when we were making the investigation. I know you know about it because you have testified about it. You've studied the commission. . . . I was thinking we've got to reform that, to turn it inside out and get it to be a good department. . . . Women are going to vote from now on. . . . I thought that I ought to bring women into the political picture in my administration. I thought about you. . . . When you were appearing before committees, you had something to say. You said it quick, you said it clear, and I could understand it. I knew, too, what you said was true—I could rely on it.

Perkins left thinking she would take the job. But first, she had to talk it over with Florence Kelley. "Glory be!" Kelley proclaimed, raising her arms to the heavens. "You don't mean it! I never thought I would live to see the day when someone we had trained, who knew about industrial conditions, cared about women, cared to have things right, would have the chance to be an administrative officer."

On January 14, 1919, Smith announced Perkins's appointment to the Industrial Commission, subject to confirmation by the Republican-controlled State Senate. The first resistance was over her name. Perkins met with a lawyer to confirm that a married woman was not legally bound to use her husband's name. Then a Democratic district leader reported to the governor that Perkins was not registered as a Democrat. After a stern talk from Smith, Perkins changed her nonpartisan status to Democrat. She had always believed that politics was merely a means to an end. Like so many of her friends, she had joined the Socialist party in Philadelphia in 1907, paying dues through 1912. Labor officials complained that she was not a union member. In the end, however, Smith's solid support proved decisive. There were four members and one chairman in the Industrial Commission. Perkins would replace one member who was retiring.

Frances Perkins dressed with what became her signature style for the rest of her career. (Library of Congress)

Perkins decided to resign from her position at the Maternity Center Association. Around the same time, she also changed her wardrobe. Up to this point, she had worn shirtwaists, tailored white blouses, and long dark skirts like most other young women. She had always chosen stylish, high-quality clothes. Now she adopted a kind of uniform—a simple black dress with a touch of white at the neck and a string of pearls around her throat. She also wore a small dark tricorn hat, which she usually kept on all day.

It did not take long before Perkins had an opportunity to put her imprint on the Industrial Commission. Early in June, in Rome, New York, 4,400 workers went on strike. Most were Italian immigrants. The workers were striking five companies—manufacturers of copper tubing, wire sheathing, screening, and boilers. The strikers wanted an eight-hour day and a raise in wages to the level that Connecticut copper companies were paying, but the owners of the mills refused to negotiate.

The strike lasted through June and into July. One of her duties on the Commission was to chair the Bureau of Mediation and Arbitration. Although she was not required to go to Rome and become involved in the dispute, she and Smith thought her presence might help end the strike sooner and avert violence. Taking such an active role in mediating labor disputes signaled that the new administration could not be counted on to automatically intervene on the side of management. Perkins was about to face her first test in her new job.

When Perkins and Packy Downey, a mediator for the bureau, arrived in Rome, the train conductor refused to let them exit because there had been gunfire in the area. They finally managed to leave the train and find a taxi. The taxi driver slid back the canvas top of his touring car so Perkins and Downey could stand up. When the taxi driver drove onto the middle of a bridge, Perkins could see a crowd of workers gathered at the far end, blocking the road. She saw rocks and partially concealed weapons in their hands.

As they approached the crowd, Downey introduced Perkins as a member of the Industrial Commission of New York State. In a brief speech, Perkins said she wanted to talk with the workers and to hear their demands. Then she would talk with the employers. The men let the taxi through to Stanwix Hall, a hotel in the center of town. Perkins spent the next few days talking with workers and the owners. From what Perkins could tell, the owners seemed genuinely upset over the strike's effect on the town and were anxious to settle, but they refused to negotiate with workers.

At the center of the conflict was James A. Spargo, the owner of the Spargo Wire Company. A strong, stocky, volatile man, he had fired a gun at strikers who tried to stop his car. When a committee of three workmen attempted to present its demands to him, Spargo knocked the men down a flight of stairs. Later, a group of Spargo's workers sent him a proposal that was returned to them through the mail, torn into pieces, with a nasty note: "Kiss my ass and go to hell."

Other employers did not want to be associated with Spargo, but they were united in refusing to meet with a committee of workers. They did not want to do anything that would seem to acknowledge the union as legitimate. The situation dragged on for a month. The town was losing more than $100,000 a week in wages, workers were living on credit, and some businesses were already ruined. Then, on July 14, someone tried to attack Spargo with a knife. The mayor called in state police.

Perkins phoned Albany to urge Governor Smith to withdraw the police, insisting there would only be more violence if they stayed. She told Smith that she would send the entire commission to Rome to hold hearings if necessary—maybe that would force employers and strikers into the same room to talk. The presence of the state police, she believed, only made an already tense situation worse. In other strikes, terrible violence had erupted when outside law enforcement was brought in.

Perkins orchestrated a deal. Knowing that strikers had a hidden cache of dynamite, she convinced them to offer it up in exchange for having the state police withdrawn. The men went down into their cellars and came up with dynamite stored in sacks and suitcases, even in a baby carriage, all of which they brought to the canal and dumped. In the end, the police withdrew and left Rome.

Her next ploy was calculated to put pressure on the factory owners. Perkins found out that Spargo had written a letter cursing his workers in coarse language. Perkins boasted to an assembled group of owners that she had the letter in her purse and was prepared to read it out loud in public. Rather than face that humiliation, the owners agreed to negotiate with the workers.

In the end, the Industrial Commission held public hearings, and employers agreed to enough concessions to end the strike. The employers refused to talk, instead letting their lawyers do the negotiating. Perkins believed the violence typical of strikes often sprang from this refusal of owners to acknowledge unions. Nevertheless, she and her colleagues counted the events in Rome an overall success.

In Albany, Perkins gave Governor Smith a full report, including details about the dynamite. "You sure had your nerve," Smith remarked. "It was a risky business, but now it's all over and I congratulate you, Commissioner."

In 1920 Smith ran for reelection as governor, which was then a two-year position. It was a bad year for Democrats throughout the country and Smith was defeated. Although in the past most members of the Industrial Commission kept their positions until they retired, the new governor appointed another commissioner to replace Perkins. The next year she took a job as executive director of the Council on Immigrant Education in New York. She organized programs to help newly arrived immigrants adjust to life in the United States.

Smith ran for governor again in 1922, and Perkins worked in his campaign. She gave speeches and organized women voters. Smith had supported female suffrage, and the ratification of the nineteenth amendment in 1920, which allowed women to vote. Smith won by a landslide.

Perkins wrote that year in her class letter for Mount Holyoke that she was reappointed by Governor Smith to her old post on the Industrial Commission, and that she was happy to have challenging, important work to do. In 1926, Smith appointed Perkins as chairman. Her reputation as a reformer was growing along with Smith's.

The Progressive Party had collapsed by then and the Democrats, more than the Republicans, had picked up their ideas. In 1916, President Wilson had persuaded Congress to enact a workmen's compensation law for federal civil servants, to exclude products of child labor from interstate commerce, and to establish an eight-hour work day on railways. The Democrats were becoming the party of social justice. Perkins was happy to be a part of the progress.

She remained successful as a mediator in disagreements between workers and employers. One British reporter wrote, "I have met a wide range of interesting women in the United States, but none who had impressed me more than this squarely-built woman with her shrewd, alert face, keen, wide-apart eyes, and warmly human personality." In handling compensation cases, he wrote, "the people never become mere 'cases' to her. . . . I never sat under a judge who was better at getting the facts, nor swifter in apprehension of their relevance."

In one compensation case, an insurance company balked about paying money to a construction worker who had been hit on the head with a heavy bucket. The man had not been able to work since and displayed strange and sometimes inappropriate behavior. The insurance company claimed the man had been mentally unstable before the accident. Perkins listened to both sides and ordered the insurance company to compensate the man for his injuries. Still, the company was slow to pay. The confused man thought it was Perkins's fault, so he came to her office with a knife. When he could not find her, he rushed into the hall and cut the throat of the lawyer for the insurance company.

"I stepped out of the washroom, and what did I see, but a man with a knife in his hand and Mr. Geddings bleeding from the throat," Perkins said later. The man ran off, and Perkins held the wounded lawyer until police arrived. Afterwards, the complainant was arrested and committed to a mental hospital, but Perkins made sure his family received the compensation money.

Another incident occurred when Perkins was in a courtroom listening to a compensation argument. The witness, a laborer, suddenly stood and began walking toward the insurance company's agent. Perkins sensed that the laborer had a gun. She moved behind him, knocked his right arm in the air and kept it up until the guard reached them. The courtroom was shocked by Perkins's brave gesture.

1928 proved to be a difficult year for Perkins. She watched as her husband's mental health deteriorated to the point that he had to be temporarily institutionalized. When her mother came to visit in the fall, she suffered a stroke and died. Some good news, though, came when Governor Al Smith won the Democratic nomination for president of the United States. Perkins worked hard to win Smith the presidency, but he was the first Roman Catholic to win a major party nomination and faced decades of prejudice. He was unpolished and spoke with a thick New York accent, pronouncing radio "raddio" and hospital as "horspital." In an attempt to help Smith counteract his reputation as a Tammany Hall, big-city, machine politician, Perkins traveled to eleven Southern states to campaign for him. The Ku Klux Klan had announced its opposition to Smith. In some places Perkins was booed and pelted with eggs and rotten tomatoes. In good humor, she complimented the group on their aim when tomatoes hit her skirt or foot. Still, Smith lost the election to Herbert Hoover.

Although sympathetic to Smith after his defeat, Perkins was pleased when Franklin Roosevelt was elected governor of New York in 1928. She had come to like and respect Roosevelt. When she first met him at a tea dance years before, she thought that he looked down at the world from on high through his pince-nez. She believed now that his terrible fight with polio, which paralyzed his legs in August 1921, had changed him into a compassionate man.

Smith told Perkins that he encouraged the new governor to keep her on as chair of the Industrial Commission. However, Roosevelt had grander plans for Perkins.

FOUR

A Responsible Public Officer

Instead of renaming her to the Industrial Commission's board, Roosevelt asked Perkins to serve as his industrial commissioner, a cabinet-level position that came with executive duties. She would not merely be an advisor but would be responsible for the operation of the entire department of 1,800 employees.

Perkins was initially reluctant to accept the position. This actually pleased Roosevelt, for it showed that she was not overly ambitious and self-seeking. Perkins decided to take the job because she considered it her duty. She had worked for years to improve labor conditions in New York, and her new position gave her a chance to follow through on much of that experience.

Perkins was sworn in on January 14, 1929. Her twelve-year-old daughter, Susanna, and a large group of friends, including Rose Schneiderman and Mary Dewson, attended the ceremony. On January 31, 1929, more than eight hundred people gathered to honor Perkins at the Hotel Astor in New York. This new position presented her with a role that connected her to both workers and labor leaders.

New York had between three and four million workers. It was the wealthiest and most populated of the states, and thus the most powerful. The Industrial Commission was divided into the Workmen's Compensation Bureau, which adjusted claims made in connection with industrial accidents; the Division of Industrial Relations, which mediated employer-employee disputes and strikes and handled claims for unpaid wages of men and women, mostly foreign-born, who otherwise would have been defrauded by their employers; the Division of Women in Industry, which checked on working conditions for women; the Division of Inspection, which enforced laws pertaining to factories and stores, housing, sanitation, fire and accident prevention, and child labor; and the Bureau of Industrial Hygiene, which disseminated information on health hazards in industries and prescribed measures for preventing occupational diseases. Heading this complex of bureaus and divisions was a monumental job. Perkins earned an annual salary of $12,000.

Her position demanded that she be in the office every day. She spent Monday and Tuesday in Albany and the rest of the week in New York City, where she moved her family to an old apartment house on Madison Avenue. With her long hours at work, Perkins saw less of her family, but she tried to make time for Susanna. Susanna was strong, healthy, warm, and artistically inclined, like her grandmother. She attended a private school. Living in the city gave Perkins the chance to reunite with her old friend Sinclair Lewis and his wife, Dorothy Thompson, a journalist, who also lived in Greenwich Village. They often met for dinner.

At the age of forty-nine, Perkins was an intense and energetic woman. She grew to dislike the publicity that accompanied her appointment as industrial commissioner. Her speeches appeared incorrectly in newspapers. Still, her new position had many advantages. She became aware of economic conditions throughout the nation. When she took office in 1929, the U.S. appeared to be enjoying genuine prosperity. The stock market was booming and President Hoover vowed to keep the federal government from interfering in business.

This relaxation of World War I's restraints created a great change in manners, morals, and spending habits. The decade became known as the "Roaring Twenties" or "The Jazz Age" after the new, "hot" style of music. Dancing and drinking, despite the nationwide prohibition against alcohol, were the rage.

The twenties brought greater freedom and independence for women. Women were now able to vote and also began to express their independence in other ways. They cut their long hair into short bobs and bound their bosoms to appear more boyish. Dresses were shortened, sometimes to the knees, which were often rouged. Women wore more makeup and smoked openly. In this period of

Texas Guinan, the lady on the piano, operated several speakeasies like this one in New York City during the 1920s. (Courtesy of the Granger Collection.)

frantic postwar prosperity, an attitude of reckless freedom, often spurred on by bootleg liquor in speakeasies, seemed to seize the nation's urban centers.

Perkins was glad women could legally vote, but she did not approve of the knee-length dresses women wore. She continued to wear her three-cornered hats and dignified business attire. She also did not agree with the change in people's spending habits, although she was pleased to see the common workingman at last able to enjoy some of the fruits of his labor.

People seemed to have more money than before—and they were eager to spend it. And if they did not have the money today, they were convinced they would have it tomorrow. They bought goods on the credit installment plan, which required only a few dollars for a down payment; the balance of payments could be made in "easy" installments.

Credit installment buying became a new phenomenon in the economy and helped to distort the prosperity and hide the underlying problems. Automobiles rolled off the assembly lines in great numbers, and everyone wanted to

This sign explains the installment plan to any passerby in need of tires. (Library of Congress)

own a car. In 1920 seven million people owned automobiles; by 1927 this number had more than tripled. Financing these purchases on an installment basis had become big business overnight, and Perkins regarded this trend skeptically. She foresaw the danger for wage earners, totally dependent upon weekly salaries, mortgaging too much of their future incomes. What if they should become unemployed? She also worried about a small upward trend in unemployment. Information provided by the New York Bureau of Labor Statistics indicated there were many areas of unemployment within her own state. Across the nation, several million factory workers were unemployed.

Periods of industrial unemployment were nothing new. Perkins's coworkers suggested that the new numbers were due to technological change—companies needed fewer workers as they introduced new methods and machinery into their factories. But Perkins thought the trouble went deeper.

Unemployment in some industries seemed to be more long term. A 1924 Russell Sage Foundation survey revealed that seventy cities in thirty-one states showed an average of ten to twelve percent—millions of men and women—of all American wage earners, were always looking for jobs. These numbers proved that not everyone was prospering. Perkins also knew that farm prices were low, and that stocks were selling for much more than they were worth.

It was difficult for most people, including members of Hoover's cabinet, to see the danger signs amidst the apparent prosperity of the 1920s. Buying stocks or simply playing the market turned into a national craze. Every day the price of stocks crept higher on the New York Stock Exchange. Anyone who gambled in the stock market seemed to be making huge profits. But most people who sold their stock turned right around and bought more, never actually receiving any money. Their profits were only on paper.

Many people borrowed money to buy stocks, a practice called buying on margin. Buying on margin allowed an investor to buy more stock—to leverage a small amount to control a larger amount of stock. An investor had to borrow the margin money from a broker, who in turn borrowed the money from a bank, using the stock to be purchased on margin as collateral to secure the loan. Margin buying was highly profitable if the stock prices rose because it magnified the profits; but if a stock lost value, the margin was quickly wiped out and the broker, and the bank, demanded full payment immediately. Margin buying is inherently risky and its excessive practice during the 1920s destabilized the stock market system.

Bernard M. Baruch, a famous financier and advisor to presidents, began to sell all of his vast stock holdings in 1928. That same year Joseph P. Kennedy, father of future President John F. Kennedy, decided to convert all of his stocks to cash and not reinvest the money. He would later say that he decided to get out of the stock market when a shoe-shine boy offered him a stock tip. Kennedy took this as a sign that stock market speculation had reached fever pitch and that prices could go nowhere but down.

The Kennedy anecdote may be apocryphal, but several experts began to warn of danger ahead. Roger Babson, a political writer, warned in 1929, "Sooner or later a crash is coming. There may be a stampede of selling that will exceed anything the stock exchange has ever witnessed."

Seven months after Hoover was inaugurated, the catastrophe that Perkins and a few others had feared struck. In September 1929, investors began to sell stocks. The market gyrated for days before it began a gradual downward spiral. Then on October 24, "Black Thursday," the crash hit. Stock holders began selling in droves and flooded the market, drowning bankers, brokers, and get-rich-quick schemers alike. The era of "permanent prosperity" had been short lived. The deepest economic depression in U.S. history was at hand. In its wake, a flood of panic and despair soon spread across the land.

The loss of income, paired with the perception of a crisis, forced consumption to drop dramatically. Industry production slowed, and workers were sent home. Although most Americans did not have a direct stake in the stock market, they were caught in the chain reaction. Banks, many over-extended with margin and other poorly secured loans, began to fail. Some bank presidents had even used their clients' money to play the market.

Tariffs on imports from other countries were so high that foreigners would no longer sell their goods to the U.S. Those with cash on hand began hoarding it, which exacerbated the situation. Farmers burned their crops and poured milk onto highways to try to limit supply and

Six days after Black Thursday, Walter Thornton, a newly destitute stock market speculator, offers to sell his car. (Courtesy of the Granger Collection.)

lift the prices they could charge. The money they earned for the crops did not even cover the costs of raising and transporting them.

The situation continued to deteriorate for months. Manufacturers, already overstocked, could not sell their goods and were forced to close down their businesses and to discharge their workers. Thousands of people bought automobiles, furniture, phonographs, washing machines, vacuum cleaners, pianos, sewing machines, radios, and refrigerators on the credit-installment plan. When they could no longer meet their payments, these goods were repossessed, if the business that had originally sold them was still around. In many subdivisions all of the houses were for sale, but there were no buyers. Rental properties went begging, and people doubled and tripled up in small apartments to save money.

On March 30, 1930, Governor Roosevelt announced the formation of a committee on Stabilization of Industry for the Prevention of Unemployment for New York. The committee recommended unemployment insurance. The number of bank failures per month nearly tripled from 1929 to 1932. The estimated number of unemployed during the Depression rose from 1,864,000 to 13,181,000. New York City had a Municipal Lodging House for Homeless which, in 1931, provided 408,000 lodgings and 1,024,247 meals. In 1932, Roosevelt's last year as governor, it provided 889,984 lodgings and 2,688,226 meals. New York State passed the Wicks Act, Temporary Emergency Relief Administration, becoming the first state to use state money for relief.

In New York City Perkins saw women dressed in expensive clothes they bought the year before the crash rummaging through garbage cans for food and putting the scraps in paper bags to take home to their families.

The causes of the Great Depression were hotly debated and remain so to this day. Some blamed the "bubble" that resulted from the ease of borrowing money to participate in the stock market. Others saw a more structural problem caused by the uneven distribution of wealth across the nation. Five percent of the population owned thirty-three percent of the real wealth. The 27,000 wealthiest families

had as much money as the twelve million poorest families. Out of the twenty-seven million families in the U.S.,
twenty-one million earned under $3,000 a year, and six
million earned less than $1,000. With so little disposable
income, these families could not afford to buy the goods
manufactured in U.S. factories fast enough to keep the
economy running. Another explanation placed most of
the blame on the failure, or inadequacy, of the banking
system to adjust to crisis quickly enough and argued that
the worst of the Great Depression could have been avoided
if the Federal Reserve System had intervened with infu-
sions of cash early on.

Whatever the specific reason for the Great Depression,
it was clear to most that the federal government failed to
act in a timely manner. The cause of this was primarily
ideological. The core idea of the philosophy of unrestricted,
free-market capitalism, which had long held dominant in
American politics, was that government should stay out
of the economy. Classical economic theory acknowledged
that capitalism would always have ups and downs but assured that the downturns would improve over time. But
beginning in 1929 the global economy entered such a deep
and long-lasting crisis that many began to wonder if it was
time for a new economic system, or at least a reevaluation
of many of the accepted tenets of classical economics.

Initially, President Hoover hung closely to the old
models. Sometimes theory even seemed to trump reality
for him. One morning in January 1930, Perkins read in
The New York Times that President Hoover quoted federal

Department of Labor Statistics that indicated business was improving. Perkins was skeptical. Unemployment was still increasing, so how could business be improving? She began researching and discovered that the answer lay in faulty statistics released by the federal Department of Labor.

Perkins pulled a copy of the most recent report from the New York State Bureau of Labor Statistics. She studied it and then dictated a brief but detailed summary to her secretary and issued it to the press. That evening she was startled to see her name emblazoned in newspaper headlines. She had expected the statement to be printed, but did not realize it would cause such a stir.

Her report contradicted the president's. She pointed out that her monthly report was based on data gathered directly from 2,000 factories in New York State. These figures clearly revealed that unemployment was steadily rising, and had been rising for the past several months. It was unlikely that the situation in other states was much different from New York. She was convinced the New York Department of Labor was right, and the federal Department of Labor was wrong.

The newspapers presented her report as a direct challenge to President Hoover's. This worried Perkins, who had not cleared her statement with Governor Roosevelt. Roosevelt was rumored to be seeking the Democratic presidential election in the 1932 election, and Perkins worried everyone would think he was behind the story.

The next day she put through a call to Roosevelt. She apologized for any embarrassment she might have caused him. He answered with a chuckle. "Apologize!" he exclaimed, "For what? I say bully for you." Bully was a favorite word of Theodore Roosevelt's, and Franklin Roosevelt had adopted it. "Certainly I read your statement," he said, "and I think it was an excellent one. I'm not only glad you made it. I say keep up the good work!"

Newspaper editors thought the federal Department of Labor had been editing its statistics to support President Hoover's optimistic statements. Newspapers began to use the monthly statement on employment trends issued by Perkins's state Department of Labor as a more accurate barometer of employment conditions throughout the country. It was released several days before the Federal Employment Index of the United States Department of Labor.

"We're not just dealing with figures on paper," Perkins told Governor Roosevelt. "We're dealing with human beings—men, women and children who are out of work and hungry."

Governor Roosevelt agreed. With Perkins' help, he had presented several reform bills to the New York legislature. These included legislation to establish old-age pensions, unemployment insurance, and a shorter work week. The latter bill was based on the theory that if those who had jobs worked fewer hours, new jobs would open up.

In 1930, Perkins traveled to Washington, D.C. several times to testify before the Senate and House Judiciary Committee to urge them to adopt legislation on unemployment offered by Senator Robert Wagner. She and William Green, president of the American Federation of

Labor (AFL), an amalgamation of labor unions, and others also lobbied President Hoover in 1931, but he vetoed the Wagner package of bills.

That same year, Governor Roosevelt sent Perkins to England to study unemployment conditions there. He hoped she would return with facts and figures to support his proposed unemployment compensation bill. Perkins took fourteen-year-old Susanna with her.

In Britain, Perkins saw that the dole, a British compulsory system of unemployment insurance adopted in 1911, had developed into a system of charity donations to the poor. As soon as people used up their short-term unemployment benefits, the British government gave free allowances to everyone who was out of work. Both Perkins and Roosevelt disagreed with the idea of a dole. They felt that these allowances could break a worker's spirit. Perkins assured Roosevelt that people wanted to work for their money.

The U.S. had experienced depressions before, but none had ever lasted so long as the Great Depression. Unemployed workers began to lose their vigor and drive. Perkins suggested that, instead of free handouts, the government should try to create jobs. She directed the New York State Employment Service, a clearinghouse for job seekers, but there were 250 applicants for every job available. She also created a division called "Junior Jobs," a placement service of part-time jobs for boys and girls under seventeen. She used these agencies to help match people with the few jobs available. For those who could not be placed in jobs, she believed there should be state or federal relief. She also wanted to establish a fund for unemployment insurance.

Perkins also recommended the enforcement of child labor laws to keep children from taking jobs from adults at lower wages. She advocated the voluntary adoption of a five-day work week (many jobs operated on a seven-day-a-week schedule); a recommendation that workers be employed at least part-time, or a few days a week as long as possible; and an increase in old-age assistance to make it possible for elderly people to retire. These were all strategies she would be able to pursue as secretary of labor.

As the Depression deepened, and some twelve million men throughout the nation were without jobs, the suicide rate for males rose dramatically. People continued to go hungry; once-proud workers stood in breadlines. Even in big cities people cultivated every spare inch of soil to grow vegetables. The price of beefsteak fell from sixty cents a pound to nineteen cents a pound, but few people had nineteen cents in their pockets. The price of wheat and flour fell to all-time lows.

Perkins believed that the federal government could institute a nationwide recovery program, but she knew the initiative for such a change in governing ideology would never come from President Hoover. Governor Roosevelt was being urged by the Democratic Party to run against Hoover in the 1932 election. Perkins knew that he would accept the challenge, and she was convinced a Roosevelt victory would be the best outcome for millions of suffering Americans.

FIVE

The Struggle for National Recovery

As secretary of labor, Perkins worked her staff hard. But because Perkins worked harder, they seldom complained. She gave them autonomy in their jobs, but no detail escaped her attention. She rewarded them with generous praise.

In testimony before a legislative committee, Perkins spoke of the Depression in terms of human misery. She reported that many families suffered from malnutrition and predicted that the full effects would not be seen for several years. This proved to be true in the medical examinations of enlisted men in World War II, as the negative effects of the poverty was still evident in their physical health.

When asked, "What do you regard as the most serious of the problems demanding attention?" Perkins answered:

A New York City soup kitchen in 1931, before Roosevelt began his new legislation.
(Courtesy of the Granger Collection.)

The human one of no work, no wages, no buying power is the most crucial. Our present social organization rests upon industrial mass production, and mass production has as its corollary mass consumption. . . . When the family pocketbook is empty, the neighborhood stores are empty. . . . The wheels stop, more workers are laid off or cut to lower than subsistence wages, so that they are also forced to stop buying . . . a general paralysis ensues. The spring of economic life dries up at its source.

Newspapers came to be called "Hoover blankets" because they were the only cover for people sleeping in parks. Whole camps of people lived in makeshift shack or tent settlements called "Hoovervilles." Hoover took the blame for the poverty, although the seeds of the Depression had been planted before he was president. Hoover eventually agreed to let the federal government intervene in the economy. He signed the Federal Home Loan Act of 1932 and created the Reconstruction Finance Corporation, which gave grants to states for relief, and increased public works, such as the Hoover Dam in Colorado, but it was too little, too late.

By 1932 unemployment had soared to a record high, and wages declined to about 60 percent less than the year before. Angry veterans of World War I, calling themselves the Bonus Army, brought their families and built camps in Washington. Unemployed, hungry people without homes, jobs, food, or decent clothes, the veterans demanded that Congress pay them the "bonus" they had been promised, but Congress refused. President Hoover ordered the U.S. Army to drive the veterans out of the camps.

By this time, the country was fed up with Hoover and the ongoing depression. The people of the U.S. were ready for a new leader. Roosevelt decided to run against Hoover in the 1932 presidential election. The months between Roosevelt's nomination and the election were difficult for Perkins. For several years her husband had managed to keep his drinking and bipolar illness under control. He attended dinner parties at friends' homes and had even been invited to the Executive Mansion in Albany. He tried to be a good father to Susanna. But in 1932 his health worsened, and Perkins hospitalized him for extended periods at a time. Over the next years she allowed little to interfere with her weekly visits to see him, but she ceased to talk about him with others. Instead, she turned toward her work.

On November 8, 1932, Roosevelt was elected president in a landslide victory over Herbert Hoover. The Democratic Party platform pledged that it wanted state-mandated unemployment insurance and old-age pensions. Perkins thought the election in the fall of 1932 was a vote against the Depression. People, insecure and frightened by the standard of living to which their lives had fallen, voted overwhelmingly for what Roosevelt had called a "New Deal" during his speech accepting the nomination at the Democratic Convention that summer.

Perkins wrote that the "New Deal" meant that the forgotten man was going to be dealt better cards. The "New Deal" expressed a changed attitude, but it was not a program. Roosevelt did not arrive in Washington with an organized, fixed plan. Instead, he committed himself to a new philosophy toward government. He believed in the notion that the nation was a community of shared interests and that government could be an instrument for public good.

When Perkins heard rumors that Roosevelt planned to appoint her to the post of secretary of labor, Perkins denied that she had started them. She insisted that he appoint someone from a labor union instead. However, Mary Dewson, the director of the Women's Democratic National Campaign Committee, thought otherwise. She worked to win Perkins the position. Even before the election, Dewson had decided that Perkins should be Roosevelt's secretary of labor. She arranged for the publication of newspaper and magazine articles about Perkins, invited her to speak at important conferences,

Franklin Delano Roosevelt, the thirty-second U.S. president, became the only man to serve more than two terms. (Courtesy of Getty Images.)

and made sure Roosevelt was inundated with letters from influential people supporting her appointment.

The possibility of Perkins' appointment was widely discussed. Leading citizens and influential newspapers and magazines, such as *The Nation,* all lent their support. Jane Addams, who had recently been awarded the Nobel Peace Prize, endorsed Perkins.

Frances Perkins's letter of appointment. (National Archives)

In February 1933, Roosevelt asked Perkins to join his cabinet, and she accepted.

> The overwhelming argument and thought which made me do it in the end in spite of personal difficulties was the realization that the door might not be opened to a woman again for a long, long time, and that I had a kind of duty to other women to walk in and sit down on the chair that was offered, and so establish the right of others long hence and far distant to sit in the high seat.

Perkins new stint was not popular everywhere. William Green, president of the AFL, said, "Labor can never become reconciled to the selection." On the whole, however, she was well received by the public.

For the inauguration ceremony, Perkins wore a long-sleeved black satin tunic dress with a soft chiffon collar beneath her tweed coat. After the swearing-in ceremonies at the White House, she attended the Inaugural Ball with Susanna. She had been too busy to shop for a ball gown herself, but her teen-aged daughter insisted that her mother have a new gown. Susanna and one of her friends went on a shopping spree. Susanna knew the dress could not be too fancy. It would be just as her mother would order it, rather staid, with just a dash of style and a discreet touch of feminine appeal. The dress was precisely that—black lace with brilliants glittering around the décolletage. Perkins was more than pleased to wear it to the ball.

While Perkins lived in Washington, D.C., she remained cautious about her daughter. Perkins kept her apartment in New York so Susanna would not have to change schools. Susanna lived there with a housekeeper, her stubby-tailed Irish terrier, and her father—when he was well. Perkins visited every weekend she could.

In Washington, Mary Harriman Rumsey, an activist and close friend of Perkins, suggested that they share a house. Perkins, who lived mostly off her modest government salary, agreed. Rumsey found an attractive, small, octagonal house in the Georgetown section of Washington, furnished it, and paid for a staff of household workers. Perkins insisted on contributing what she could toward expenses. The move close to her job proved beneficial, as she was about to take on an even heavier load.

SIX

Making the New Deal Work

In the months between Roosevelt's election and his inauguration, economic conditions had worsened at such a frightening pace that it prompted Congress to pass the twentieth amendment to the Constitution, which moved the date of inauguration up from March 4th to January 20th. As the country waited for the new president to take office, banks collapsed, businesses failed, and farms were foreclosed.

The Hoover Administration had been hesitant to use the federal government in an attempt to end the depression or to alleviate the suffering it caused. Roosevelt planned to push legislation through the Democratic-controlled Congress that would actively tackle the economic crisis. He did not profess to have a cohesive plan. He proposed constant experimentation—to try any measure he thought would help. If it worked, he would continue the program; if

This cartoon from 1933 shows Franklin Roosevelt pulling Congress and the entire country down the road to emergency legislation. (Courtesy of the Granger Collection.)

it failed, he would throw it out and try something else.

After taking the oath of office, Roosevelt began his dramatic and productive first hundred days in office. He worked closely with cabinet members, his aides, outside economists, professors, reporters, and others to craft several pieces of legislation that forever altered the relationship between the citizens of the United States, business, and government. Perkins was involved in several of the most critical decisions.

Before she could help President Roosevelt fight the Great Depression, Perkins had to learn her way around the Department of Labor and to staff it with the best qualified people. To begin with, there was the problem of her title. Because she was the first woman to hold a cabinet post, reporters and others were unsure of how to address her. Noting that male cabinet members were addressed as "Mr. Secretary," she suggested they call her "Madam Secretary."

As secretary of labor, Perkins soon realized she had inherited a disorganized and largely untended bureaucracy. No one seemed to know who occupied which rooms, or where to find important files or records amid the dirty, cockroach-infested offices. She saw no work schedule, programs, or work plans left behind by her predecessor, even though the country was in the grip of economic calamity.

Clearly, she had her work cut out. One of the first things Perkins did was abolish the racially segregated lunchrooms and disband the spy system. The Bureau of Immigration was then part of the Labor Department, and she did away with the use of strong-armed tactics to track down and deport aliens. She appointed Daniel MacCormack, formerly president of a large New York bank, as head of the Bureau of Immigration.

Perkins also announced the reorganization of the Bureau of Labor Statistics and hired Isador Lubin, a young statistician from the Brookings Institute, to head it. He was an affable man who became one of Perkins's principal aides and supporters. Soon the bureau was producing accurate information about employment, living costs, prices, wages, and other aspects of the economy.

Perkins retained Grace Abbott, the chief of the Children's Bureau, and Abbott's assistant, although both were Republicans. Abbott was a tall, vibrant woman who had been a member of the Consumers League in New York and was considered for the position of Secretary of Labor under Hoover. When Perkins arrived in Washington, Abbott arranged for her to be introduced to senators and representatives on Capitol Hill. Abbott shared Perkins' desire to abolish child labor and to improve the operation of the Children's Bureau.

Perkins created a nationwide system of free employment agencies known as the United States Employment Service. Within four years, nineteen million people found jobs through this service. Unemployment for black workers was 30 to 60 percent higher than for whites. She prohibited the Employment Service from racially discriminating against job seekers and then hired Lawrence Oxley, the first African-American man to hold an executive position in the Department of Labor. He had studied at Harvard and had been special investigator with the War Department Commission on Training Camp Activities.

At her first cabinet meeting, Perkins announced that she had called a conference of labor leaders and experts to draft recommendations for unemployment relief. She said a program of public works should be one of the first steps.

A U.S. Employment Services advertisement at Buffalo, New York in 1943. (Library of Congress)

One large political issue hung over all discussions on how to fight the depression. The U.S. Constitution established a system in which the national government and the state governments share power and responsibility. The next decision would be choosing the number of programs, such as unemployment insurance, that Perkins and Roosevelt wanted to put into place. Would the states or the federal government be responsible for the programs? If the federal government funded the program should it turn over the operation to states, or was it their responsibility to see that the money was spent as the federal government mandated? These questions are still debated today, but in 1933, many of them were being asked for the first time.

Shortly after Inauguration Day, Harry Hopkins and William Hodson came down from New York to see Perkins. Hopkins was chairman of the New York State Temporary Relief Administration, which had been established by Roosevelt when he was governor. Hodson was director of the Welfare Council of New York City. They wanted to present their ideas for how the federal government should tackle unemployment. Although there were hundreds of plans in circulation, Perkins had worked with Hopkins and Hodson in New York and wanted to hear what they had to say. The three met at the Women's University Club in a cubbyhole under the stairs, where the men laid out a plan. They suggested that the federal government provide funds to the states. Because most states had already set up organizations to dispense unemployment relief to workers, this method would be faster and, if properly regulated from Washington, could create a new model of federal and state cooperation. Hopkins and Hodson impressed Perkins with the exactness of their knowledge and the practical details of their plan.

The men told her they had not been able to see the president. Perkins made an appointment for them to see Roosevelt. The president listened with interest to their presentation and then called in Senator Wagner, as well as Senators Robert LaFollette of Wisconsin and Edward Costigan of Colorado, and asked them to draw up a bill to establish the Federal Emergency Relief Administration (FERA) based on Hopkins and Hodson's plan.

Distributing relief money to the unemployed was one

tactic Roosevelt and Perkins tried; reemploying them in the service of the federal government would be another. They called for a new program that combined one of the president's deepest concerns—conservation—with job relief.

The Civilian Conservation Corps (CCC) offered young men aged seventeen to twenty-three food and clothing, board, medical care, and a dollar-a-day stipend in exchange for working at jobs to clean up and improve the national parks and forests. The young men would live in camps similar to military bases and build wildlife shelters, picnic areas, and other facilities in existing national parks. They would also dig canals, restore historic battlefields, stock rivers and lakes with fish, clear beaches and campgrounds, and plant trees. Plaques acknowledging the workers can still be found in U.S. national parks and forests.

The men earned $30 a month, $22 of which went to their families. In addition to room, board, and medical and dental care, they received clothing and necessary transportation without charge. For some of the young men, the CCC provided them their first pair of shoes. Leaders earned $45 a month and their assistants $36.

Perkins suggested that the U.S. Army be assigned to take care of the men going into the woods, and that the Department of Agriculture and the Forestry Service could decide which projects they worked on. Roosevelt asked Perkins to use the Labor Department to recruit the men and she asked the army to call back unemployed reserve officers to help.

The CCC also set up camps for unemployed young

women, but there were only 8,500 women in the program, compared to 2.5 million men. The first female camp, Camp Jane Addams, was set up in Bear Mountain Park in New York to teach unemployed women homemaking skills and personal hygiene. Eleanor Roosevelt and Perkins acted as advocates for the camps for unemployed women.

Perkins was proud of the CCC and the work it did. Thousands of families were able to remove their names from the local relief rolls. Enrollees regained self-respect and self-confidence and benefited both physically and mentally. Decades later, a group of prosperous men would personally testify to Perkins how much the CCC had done for them in the troubled years of their youth.

Perkins was also involved in the development of the Federal Emergency Relief Administration (FERA), which gave matching grants to states to provide food, clothing, fuel, medicine, housing, and other necessities for the unemployed.

When her daughter, Susanna, who was eighteen at the time, complained that most public buildings looked dreary and gloomy and suggested that artists decorate their walls, Perkins thought it was a great idea. She mentioned the idea to Roosevelt, who saw it as a way to put artists to work doing something besides digging ditches and planting trees. Perkins put her idea to the test by borrowing 130 oil paintings from the Corcoran Gallery and mounting them on the walls of the Labor Building.

As Roosevelt neared the end of his first one hundred days in office, Congress passed the National Industrial Recovery Act (NIRA). Perkins worked long hours helping to draft the legislation. The NIRA included a federal public works program called the Public Works Administration (PWA) that provided jobs for the unemployed by hiring them to work on public construction projects. Projects built by PWA workers included the Lincoln Tunnel and LaGuardia Airport in New York, the Overseas Highway in Florida, the San Francisco-Oakland Bay Bridge, as well as schools, roads, and even aircraft carriers and cruisers for the navy.

The use of government funds to create jobs turned out to be controversial. Critics complained that the new jobs were not necessary, but were "made" work. Perkins strongly disagreed. She argued that every dollar spent on public works created four dollars worth of national income.

Perkins's idea that each dollar of public money spent created four dollars of national income was adapted from British economist John Maynard Keynes, who met with Roosevelt in 1934 to discuss his ideas. Keynes argued that in economic downturns private businesses slow or stop investment and concentrate on preserving their capital, which meant it was up to governments to generate activity by running up deficits. While the president was influenced by Keynes's theories, he never fully accepted the idea that an unbalanced budget could have positive consequences. Today, some economists argue that it was Roosevelt's failure to fully accept Keynes's ideas and his continuing efforts to balance the federal budget that extended the Great Depression throughout the decade.

The NIRA also established the National Recovery Administration (NRA), which was intended to stabilize wages and prices by working with industries and workers to develop guidelines for wages and prices. The NRA also helped to protect workers who formed unions. It selected the Blue Eagle, a fierce bird that is a cross between the American Eagle and a Native American symbol, as its emblem. Perkins wrote "there was a great lift in the spirit of the people as they marched in parades [or] proudly displayed the Blue Eagle in their windows."

When the steel industry developed one of the first NRA codes, Perkins decided to visit some steel factories. In Homestead, Pennsylvania, the site of a bloody strike

U.S. businesses showed their support by hanging a NRA sign in their window. (Courtesy of the Franklin Delano Roosevelt Library.)

in 1892, she arranged a meeting in the Hall of Burgesses. When the mayor refused to let some men enter because they were accused of being Communists, Perkins insisted on speaking with them. When the mayor and the steel company police forbade her from communicating with them in a public park, she went to the post office, which was federally controlled. There she met with the men and invited them to testify at a public hearing in Washington.

Beginning in the decades after the Civil War, American workers who had tried to form unions to negotiate with business owners and managers had met fierce and often violent resistance. The American Federation of Labor, an umbrella group for unions, formed in 1881 to help sort out conflicts with owners, but employers continued to resist unionization. Some would not hire union workers and harassed workers who decided to join unions. Most owners and conservative politicians insisted that unions could not legally represent workers. From their perspective, each worker had the right to sell his or her labor at the highest price. They did not have to take a job and could quit at any time. Unions violated this principle by standing between the companies and the individual worker. The owners also argued that the factories were their property, and they had full right to operate their property in the way they chose. To force them to agree to union demands was an illegal and unfair restriction of their property rights.

For years the arguments of owners carried the day. It helped that most elected officials were supported by wealthy business owners and industrialists. But as more people were forced to go to work in factories, this philosophy began to change. In 1914 Congress passed the Clayton Anti-Trust Act, which stated that unions had the right to exist. However, during the Great Depression workers were afraid to try to organize because there were so few jobs. The NIRA protected a worker's right to organize. Soon, a series of strikes swept the nation.

The 1930s was marked by conflicts between workers and employers. One of the most difficult was a strike of longshoremen in San Francisco. When the shipping companies refused to deal with the union, workers in other unions—truckers, cooks, fire fighters, pilots, and engineers—supported the longshoremen by going out on strike. Then, on what came to be known as Bloody Thursday, violence broke out between the strikers and police. Two men were killed and seventy-three seriously injured. The following Monday, 15,000 workers marched in San Francisco.

President Roosevelt was in Hawaii. Secretary of State Cordell Hull thought federal troops should be sent in to break up the strike, but Perkins protested. "I call it serious for us to use troops against American citizens who . . . haven't committed murder or rioted. They haven't interfered with the U.S. mail. . . . I cannot tell you how serious it would be . . . for the basic labor-industry and labor-government relationships of the country if we were to do this."

When contacted, Roosevelt wired that he supported Perkins and gave her authority to speak for him. Roosevelt trusted Perkins in labor matters. She worked to calm the workers and within a week the strike was over.

A witness watches policemen fire on striking longshoremen in San Francisco on Bloody Thursday. (Library of Congress)

During the twelve years that Perkins was labor secretary, she worked with and helped settle many labor disputes. Not surprisingly, she was criticized as being too pro-labor, but she never wavered in her insistence that strikes and disputes should be settled by negotiation, conciliation, and mutual agreement—not force. In her oral history she stated, "There have been two-fisted males in this office and strikes were never prevented. . . . It's doubtful if any clear-thinking citizen would be willing to give any agency of government the absolute power to interfere with other citizens."

Because she usually sided with labor, employers accused her of encouraging union violence. They said that if the workers knew the federal government would crack down on them they would not strike so often. Newspaper articles and letters vilified her as "Princess Pinkie" and "Mrs. Hitler." She was accused of being a Communist by citizens and some legislators. It was a charge that would follow her for years.

Perkins thought her department should set workplace guidelines. In July 1934, she and Clara Beyer created the Division of Labor Standards (DLS) to address problems of health, safety, and working conditions. Clara Beyer was a trained economist who graduated from the University of California and had taught at Bryn Mawr. She previously worked as the executive secretary of the New York Consumers League.

That same year, Henry Ford, president of the Ford Motor Company, demonstrated his confidence in America's economic recovery by restoring the "five dollars a day" minimum wage in his automobile factories.

Perkins continued to live a hectic life. She held press conferences, wrote articles, gave interviews, chaired meetings and attended conventions to educate people about the need for social legislation and labor reform. She also spoke on the radio. A voluble and exceptional speaker, Perkins was able to explain complicated issues in easy-to-understand terms. A poll of Washington broadcasters named Perkins among the five best political speakers in the country. She was pictured on the cover of *Time* magazine on August 14, 1933, and numerous cartoons of her appeared in national newspapers. She wrote articles for *Collier's*, a very

The August 14, 1933, issue of Time *Magazine features Perkins on the cover. In the article "Truce at a Crisis," her work is applauded and her appointment affirmed because of her handling of the steel strikes.* (Time, Inc.)

popular magazine, and was dubbed "Fearless Perkins" or "Ma Perkins" in the press after a popular daytime radio soap opera. Ma Perkins on the program solved numerous problems of people in her hometown. Even cabinet members called her "Ma Perkins" until Roosevelt chided them.

SEVEN

Social
Security

The Roosevelt administration continued to push anti-poverty legislation well past the first one hundred days of Roosevelt's presidency. Perkins continued to be a part of the effort for years. In late 1933 and early 1934, she worked hard to achieve two more of her goals—to establish unemployment insurance and old-age insurance. She had been talking about the need for these two programs for years and the American people were now more inclined to agree with her. She spoke of the need for these programs, and the necessity for people to have a sense of economic security, in her book *People at Work*, which was published in 1934.

People at Work was stitched together by a journalist friend, Martha Bensley Bruere, from Perkins's articles and speeches. Perkins was not happy with the result, however,

Perkins and Roosevelt shared many of the same principles and maintained a rewarding long-term working relationship. (Department of Labor)

and reconstructed it with the help of an editor from the publishing house. In the end, the book had nine chapters covering the history of American labor from colonial times to the Great Depression.

Perkins was now one of the most famous members of the Roosevelt administration, and one of the most controversial. The chauffeur-driven car she traveled in did not have a labor department seal on the door, but this did not deter reporters. During one stay at a hotel a throng of photographers and reporters made it almost impossible for her to open the door. She finally was able to push it open enough to yell out that the actress Greta Garbo was in the lobby. The reporters hurried away and she got to her meeting on time.

In the summer of 1934 Roosevelt created the Committee on Economic Security (CES), composed of cabinet members. Roosevelt wanted the CES to develop a comprehensive social security program for workers that included unemployment insurance and old-age insurance. He insisted that Perkins chair the committee: "You care about this thing. You believe in it. Therefore I know you will put your back to it more than anyone else, and you will drive it through."

Chairing the CES was the culmination of a lifetime's work for Perkins. She and the president agreed that the committee should take a broad approach to the issue of economic security for all workers. There was both a humanitarian and practical reason for this expansive view. The humanitarian approach was obvious. Millions of men and women had entered the ranks of the long-term unemployed since 1929 and they needed immediate relief. The more practical reason was that relief checks might help to restart the economy by giving money to would-be consumers. Old-age pensions would have the same humanitarian impact. However, in addition to the practical effect of helping to prime the pump of the stagnant economy, it would also take many older workers out of the job market. Perkins and Roosevelt were convinced that a surplus of workers was working to depress wages and limit labor's ability to negotiate for higher wages and better working conditions.

A family, fleeing the Depression, is forced to sell their trailer and belongings for food on a New Mexico Highway. (Library of Congress)

Roosevelt saw the work of the CES as the culmination of his plans. He wanted a system that helped protect all American workers throughout their lives. Perkins, however, was troubled by how to administer a program of life-long, universal coverage.

In addition to the big questions of unemployment compensation and old-age assistance, the CES also reported on the status of health insurance, workmen's compensation, and specialized types of public assistance for specific groups, such as the handicapped and dependent children. "As I see it," Perkins observed, "we shall have to establish in this country substantially all of the social-insurance measures which the western European countries have set up in the last generation." But she warned that social insurance alone could not "promise anything like complete economic security. More important than all social-insurance devices together is employment."

For months Perkins accumulated statistics and studied plans of other countries. The biggest problem was how to pay for it. She was also concerned that the social security plan might be declared unconstitutional by the U.S. Supreme Court. There was a great deal of opposition to social insurance. Much of it came from bankers and insurance companies who feared social insurance would hurt their business. Even some social workers feared that a social security program that reduced poverty would put them out of work. Others argued that social welfare programs destroyed initiative, discouraged thrift and stifled individual responsibility. Perkins explained that social security was only part of a retirement plan that should also include individual savings and company pensions.

Other countries and some states had set up social insurance plans of their own, giving Perkins and the CES some models of how such a system might work. Germany set up social insurance systems in 1883, and eighteen states had some form of old-age pensions. I. M. Rubinow, an American expert, traced the background of social insurance in Europe. He set forth the theoretical justification for a social security system in his 1913 book *Social Insurance* that Perkins studied. Wisconsin already had an unemployment compensation plan that influenced founding principles of the CES. The Bull Moose Party of 1912, as well as the Prohibition Party, Farmer-Labor Party, and the Socialist Party, supported social insurance in presidential elections since 1900.

Roosevelt thought the social security program should be presented in a single legislative package covering both unemployment and old-age insurance. He wanted it to be a state-federal program financed by contributions from employees and employers instead of from general tax revenues.

Supreme Court Justice Brandeis suggested funding both parts of the plan with a payroll tax on employers. Then the amount employers are taxed to fund the plans could be deducted from their federal tax. This seemed a good approach to Perkins, and Roosevelt agreed. The president knew that funding it by payroll taxes would protect it from future politicians who wanted to destroy it, because they could not simply refuse to fund it.

At first, Perkins opposed making employees contribute. She pointed out that employers would simply shift the payroll tax to the consumer in higher prices, which effectively meant employees were already paying their share. But the committee decided that the payroll taxes were to begin in 1937 and that both employers and employees would pay 1 percent. The contributions would rise 0.5 percent each of the next three years. A worker's benefits were determined by the total amount of wages on which they had paid taxes, without a means test or proof of financial need. The reserve fund would be invested in U.S. government bonds and administered by a Social Security Board.

There was still the problem of national unemployment insurance. Frustrated at their inability to resolve the issues, Perkins developed a plan. One day during Christmas week she called the committee working on the plan to meet at her house at 8:00 PM, disconnected all telephone service, and told the servants to turn away all visitors. She would provide a bottle of spirits and they would sit up all night, if necessary, until they decided the thorny question once and for all. The committee worked until two in the morning before agreeing that the individual, as well as the employer, would make contributions and that the pay-out of the benefit would be based on the individual's previous earnings. When Roosevelt received their report, he insisted the tax rate start at 2 percent and that it rise to 6 percent in twelve years. This would insure the program's solvency through 1965. He then sent legislation to Congress based on the CES report.

The plan underwent changes in Congress. The Social Security Act that was finally passed contained ten programs, including public assistance to the blind and children without parental support. The plan was popular with most of the public, but its enemies were virulent. Even one of Roosevelt's top advisors, Raymond Moley, the nominal leader of the famous group of aides called the Brain Trust, resigned because he thought unemployment insurance would destroy individual initiative.

The impact of the Social Security Act was profound and continues to be so to this day. No government bureau touches the lives of millions of Americans—the old, the jobless, the sick, the needy, the blind, the mothers, the children—more directly. Of all the changes that characterized the New Deal, the Social Security Act was the most dramatic break with the past. For the first time government provided its citizens protection against the hazards and vicissitudes of life.

Perkins knew the act was not perfect. Farm laborers and domestic workers were not covered, and there was no universal health insurance, primarily because of the vehement objections of doctors. Still, she could savor achieving her lifelong goal of providing old-age and unemployment insurance to American workers. Perkins continued to educate the American public on the importance of the social security program through speeches, newspaper and magazine articles, and radio addresses. She wanted all Americans to be well informed on the program's basic concepts.

At the official bill signing, Roosevelt requested a special pen for Perkins to sign the bill. Although she was supposed to be honored with the first social security number and card, Perkins hastily declined. She did not want to reveal that the Department of Labor and the FBI listed her date

Roosevelt signs the Social Security bill into law with senators, representatives and cabinet members standing around him. Senator Robert Wagner, who helped institute the NRA, stands left of Frances Perkins. (Courtesy of Mount Holyoke Archives and Special Collections.)

of birth as 1882, instead of the actual birth date of 1880. For years Perkins pretended to be two years younger than she was. Instead, a retired legal secretary, Ida Fuller of Ludlow, Vermont, became the first old-age insurance beneficiary when she received Social Security Check Number 00-000-001 on January 30, 1940.

Although many people credit Perkins with the social security program, she insisted it was the result of several people's efforts. During a speech at Cornell University she said, "It represented the thinking of 150 of the best minds in the country." However, she was proud of her part. In an interview she later said that Social Security was the best thing she had done for her country and she was honored when President Roosevelt gave her credit for the bill.

In a speech to the nation in August 1938, the third anniversary of the Social Security Act, President Roosevelt reflected on the program's beginnings. "This third anniversary would not be complete if I did not express the gratitude of the nation to those who helped me in making social security legislation possible . . . First of all, to the first woman who has ever sat in the cabinet of the United States, Miss Perkins. . . ."

This poster from 1935 urges workers to take advantage of the new Social Security Act. (Courtesy of the Granger Collection.)

After the ceremony, Perkins took a train to New York City because she received a call from her husband's nurse saying that he was missing. With the help of several friends, Perkins found Paul unharmed. Even though they spent a great deal of time apart, Perkins and Paul kept up a loving correspondence and tender regard for one another during the years that he was ill.

Back in the office, Perkins helped select people to sit on the Social Security Board, including her friend Mary Dewson. At meetings of the board Perkins sometimes held the floor with long soliloquies that allowed for no interruption. She had a rich, variegated voice accentuated by animated facial expressions and graceful hand gestures. Finally, at one meeting, Dewson interrupted: "I have an idea I should like to contribute and Mr. Wagenet, head of the Department of Unemployment Insurance, wants to make a few points." Later, Perkins apologized to Dewson for her lack of good manners. She knew short speeches were best but found it difficult to be concise with her vast accumulation of data.

In Washington, life was pleasant for a short time in the handsome corner home Perkins shared with Mary Harriman Rumsey. Rumsey was the daughter of a railroad tycoon and sister of Averell Harriman, an ambassador. Her husband was killed in an automobile accident. As a debutante, Rumsey had helped found the Junior League in New York and met Perkins when she was a young social worker. They both worked at the Maternity Center Association in New York where Rumsey was a director.

Rumsey knew every important person in Washington and had a lively interest in politics. She chaired the Consumers Advisory Board of the National Recovery Administration and promoted the formation of consumer groups across the country. They gave frequent dinner parties and invited a fascinating assortment of artists and politicians, such as sculptor Jo Davidson and photojournalist Margaret Bourke-White, who showed them recent photos she had taken of the "Dust Bowl" that was caused by the drought of the 1930s in the Midwest. Then, one day in December 1934, Mary Rumsey was seriously hurt when her horse fell on her. She later contracted pneumonia and died.

Perkins mourned the loss of her friend but had plenty on her agenda to keep her busy. She seemed to be living the life of a glamorous political figure, but out of fear for her daughter's safety and exposure of her husband's mental illness, Perkins usually avoided reporters except to report on Labor Department business. Although humble, she enjoyed the recognition of her political and social contributions. Soon, prestigious organizations and educational institutions would place Perkins under the public spotlight even more.

EIGHT

Politics
and Honor

A typical day for Perkins started at seven o'clock in the morning when she took Communion at the Episcopal Church. In her office she went through mail before conferring with state officials on labor problems. Later the bureau heads reported to her. There might be a press conference around noon, followed by individual appointments. After eating a quick lunch from a tray in her office, labor representatives approached her about particular problems, or she attended cabinet meetings or met with the Public Works Board. Later in the afternoon she usually met with a recovery or relief group and held informal conferences on special problems. She ate dinner between 7:30 and 8:30 in the evening, usually while meeting with aides. Perkins then returned to her office and worked on correspondence and reports until 10:30 PM or later.

The Department of Labor building on Constitution Avenue, where Perkins worked between 1935 and 1945. (Library of Congress)

When the Labor Department moved to a new building in 1935, a small sitting-dressing room adjoined her office. Perkins could see the Department of Agriculture greenhouses across Constitution Avenue and the gleaming Washington Monument from the small balcony. Just beyond the grass-covered park were thousands of flowering Japanese cherry trees.

In March 1935, Perkins became the first woman to deliver the Charter Day Address at the University of California. On the same day, she, Jane Addams, and Herbert Hoover received honorary degrees. Photographers asked the three honorary degree recipients to pose together for pictures, but Hoover refused to be photographed with Perkins. He still resented her attack on his unemployment statistics in 1930 and considered her an extremist.

Perkins received several honorary degrees. In June of 1933, Perkins received the degree of Doctor of Law from both Goucher College and the University of Michigan. She was named a trustee of Mount Holyoke College in 1934, and gave a Founder's Day address at her alma mater in November that same year.

At home, however, Perkins's popularity was sometimes hampered by her poor public relations skills. She was an outspoken and independent woman with power and influence who did not use her husband's name, a practice that

BY PAUL W. WARD

Madam Secretary

Perkins was the target of several unflattering articles. This composite features a sketch that appeared in the March 11, 1936, issue of The Nation. *The text, excerpted from an article by Paul W. Ward, appeared in the March 27, 1935, issue of the same publication.* (University of North Carolina at Greensboro)

Fannie is not a policy-maker and never has been one. She lacks the imagination. More especially, she lacks the courage. Despite her Woman Militant hats, she is a peace-at-any-price person except within the privacy of her own office, where she rules over the affairs of underlings with Draconian ruthlessness. In her the New Deal's chronic infection reaches an acute stage. She suffers from a middle-class mind. That—with her lack of any marrow-deep understanding of labor's problems—accounts for her willingness to assist Roosevelt in applying his Boy Scout technique to the class struggle. It accounts for her almost pathological abhorrence of publicity, her fear of conflict, the dreadful chicanery of the "social security" program she helped to engineer, and her untiring ability to rationalize and excuse the ever-increasing number of betrayals that her White House hero has meted out to labor.

Her position with respect to organized labor is like the position of many adults with respect to spinach: they appreciate the vegetable intellectually but have no stomach for it. All but a very few labor leaders find themselves unwelcome in Fannie's office. It once took William Green, A. F. of L. president, seven weeks to get an interview with her, whereas professors and social workers can get her ear at almost any time.

was radical in the 1930s. Many in the public could not accept it.

Some members of Congress, as well as the press, criticized Perkins. She usually ignored the criticism, until she heard a rumor that she was "a foreign-born Jew." The rumor stemmed from reporters who could find no record of a birth certificate for Perkins from 1882. This was the second time Perkins had to deal with the fact that she lied about her birth date. Just as before, she refused to clear up the discrepancy. What the reporters did find was a marriage certificate from a man named Paul Wilson and his wife Matilda Wadski—whom reporters insisted was Perkins. Perkins could have quickly put an end to the confusion by simply admitting she was born in Boston in 1880, but she refused.

In the meantime, Perkins faced more pressing issues. Two pieces of New Deal legislation—the National Recovery Administration (NRA) of 1933 and the Wagner Act of 1935—had created tensions between labor and management. One important section of the NRA gave laborers the legal right to organize and bargain collectively with employers over pay rates, job conditions, and other workplace issues. During the first year of the NRA, more than one million workers joined labor unions. When employers refused to recognize these unions, employees often refused to work. Strikes and violence over union recognition became widespread.

On May 27, 1935, the entire New Deal suffered a blow when the U.S. Supreme Court ruled the NRA unconstitutional on the grounds that it regulated commerce that was not interstate, which the court unanimously decided was beyond the federal government's power. The administration immediately sponsored a bill that would help fill the gap left by the Supreme Court's decision. Senator Robert Wagner, who had also introduced the Social Security Act, introduced the National Labor Relations Act. It was sometimes referred to as the Wagner Act. Wagner, the son of a janitor, was brought to America from Germany when he was nine. The youngest of six children, he was the only one who went to school. Wagner attributed his success in the new country to luck. He supported himself while attending college and law school. Perkins admired his reliance

In this 1934 cartoon, Roosevelt's detractors grumble under a Depression cloud while he sails the ship of state toward recovery with the American people on board. (Courtesy of the Granger Collection.)

on facts rather than exaggeration in his speeches. His appearance and expression were austere, and he lacked the charisma of Al Smith or Roosevelt. Nevertheless, he was repeatedly elected to represent New York in the United States Senate from 1927 to 1949.

The Wagner Act, passed in the summer of 1935, created a legal framework to guarantee workers' right to organize. It required employers to bargain with union representatives and empowered the National Labor Relations Board to supervise elections of union leaders. It also ruled that employers cannot treat union members unfairly, nor can a company sponsor a union. Union membership expanded rapidly to more than six million workers by the end of Roosevelt's first term. But the strikes continued and grew in size and violence.

As tensions rose, Perkins received threats. She kept her chin up and still marched into her office on time every morning, but Roosevelt ordered twenty-five policemen to guard Perkins at a dinner in Philadelphia where she spoke on labor problems.

After the NRA was struck down, Perkins told Roosevelt about two bills that could do everything she and Roosevelt considered important under the NRA. She kept them locked up in the lower left-hand drawer of her desk in case of such an emergency. The first bill established conditions under which goods and services purchased by the government were manufactured, including an eight-hour day, a forty-hour week, safety and health standards, a minimum wage, and the prohibition of using child workers under the age of sixteen. Known as the Walsh-Healey Public Contracts Act, it was passed in June 1936.

The second bill had a broader impact. It was known as the Wages and Hours Act, or Fair Labor Standards Act. When the bill passed in 1938, it abolished the employment of children under sixteen in interstate industry (eighteen in dangerous industries), established a minimum wage of forty cents an hour and a maximum work week of forty hours for all workers in interstate commerce. For work beyond forty hours a week, workers had to be paid "time and a half," or one-and-a-half times the hourly wage.

On November 3, 1936, Franklin Roosevelt was reelected president of the United States in a landslide victory. His running mate again was John Nance Garner. Roosevelt asked Perkins to continue as secretary of labor, but Perkins shied away from the offer. Perhaps her resignation would be the best way to end the industrial strikes that plagued the nation. Her negotiations with William Green and his powerful American Federation of Labor (AFL), as well as John L. Lewis and his Congress of Industrial Organizations (CIO), turned out to be unsuccessful. Lewis had even accused her of being "woozy in the head." Yet Roosevelt insisted Perkins work with him, and she agreed to stay on as secretary of labor.

Despite the administration's effort, and the millions of dollars pumped into the economy, recession hit in 1937-1938. 1937 proved to be a difficult year for Perkins. First, a series of "sit-down" strikes spread from the rubber tire and automobile plants in Ohio and Michigan to the Ford

Frances Perkins shakes hands with steelworkers. (Courtesy of the Franklin Delano Roosevelt Library.)

and General Motors plants in Detroit. This led to other strikes throughout the nation. The sit-down strike was a new technique adopted by workers who not only refused to work, but also refused to leave the factories in an attempt to avoid being replaced.

Workers threatened walkouts in several steel companies, including Republic, Inland, and Youngstown Sheet and Tube. Perkins tried to mediate agreements. She visited the steel mills and talked with dozens of the workmen, many of whom were stripped to the waist in the blistering heat from the blast furnaces. Perkins charmed the workers when she had lunch with them in the workers' cafeteria and flipped a coin with one of the bosses to see who would pay the check.

Perkins tried to bring William Green, the head of the AFL, and the steel barons together to work out an agreement and avoid a major steel strike. But the steel company operators refused to even be introduced to Green. They worried that the stockholders in their companies would accuse them of collaborating with the enemy. William Green stormed out of the meeting in a huff, leaving Perkins incredibly embarrassed.

But positive things were happening outside of Perkins's work life. Early in Susanna's junior year of college, she left Bryn Mawr in Pennsylvania to work in Washington, D.C. as an assistant at the Phillips Art Gallery. She was engaged to David M. Hare, the son of one of Perkins's friends. Perkins announced the engagement in December 1936, on Susanna's twentieth birthday. On March 12, 1938, Susanna and David were married. They soon left for Santa Fe, New Mexico, where David started preparing a photo book on the Pueblo Indians.

In May 1938, a group called the Committee on Un-American Activities was formed in the House of Representatives to investigate possible Communist activity in America. Representative Martin Dies was named chairman. Dies claimed that Communists controlled at least 280 labor unions and 483 newspapers. One of his first targets was Harry Bridges, a longshoreman and labor leader, who was originally from Australia. Dies put pressure on Perkins to

The Washington Post *from January 25, 1939, features the article* (center) *"Miss Perkins Asks Hearing On Charges." The House Committee on Un-American Activities and chairmen Dies and Thomas were precursors to the anticommunist McCarthyism of the 1940s and '50s.* (University of North Carolina at Greensboro)

have Bridges deported, but she could find no evidence that Bridges was a Communist. Then, on January 24, 1939, J. Parnell Thomas, a representative from New Jersey, introduced a forty-page resolution of impeachment against Perkins and two of her staff members, charging them with failing to enforce the immigration laws.

Perkins volunteered to appear before the House Judiciary Committee where she discussed the Bridges case in detail and asked the committee "to protect me and to secure my rights and my reputation if I have done no wrong." Roosevelt was a master of public relations who could easily deflect most political attacks. It was much easier to attack one of his assistants.

On March 24, 1939, the committee issued a report that there was not enough factual evidence presented to support the resolution of impeachment, and all charges were dropped.

People continued to whisper behind Perkins's back. Eleanor Roosevelt wrote to a mutual friend:

> I realize that Frances is under a strain and I wish she could take it more lightly because . . . it is purely a political attack. . . . At present, many of the Federation of Women's Clubs members are down . . . on Frances because they believe she is a Communist. When you get women started along those lines they are like sheep. They think Dies is doing a wonderful job and do not realize that he is doing something to make himself personally popular with the sole idea of being candidate for President, and Miss Perkins was the easiest victim.

As much as the committee wanted to oust Perkins, the worst gossip it could come up with was that Perkins sometimes played poker with President Roosevelt, Postmaster General James Farley, and Senator Robert Wagner.

Her opponents continued to insist that Perkins was of Russian-Jewish ancestry. In a speech to the House, Congressman Phillip A. Bennett of Missouri referred to "Frances Wadski Perkins" and to her "native Russia." She asked him to correct the Congressional Record. Bennett amended his comments about her birth, marriage, and national heritage, but not about her being "surrounded by Communists."

Perkins did her best to dispel the rumors and said there were no Jews in her ancestry. She insisted, "If I were a Jew, I would make no secret of it. On the contrary, I would be proud to acknowledge it." Then she proceeded to give the wrong birth date and correct marriage record. An investigator for the Daughters of the American Revolution (D.A.R.) hired a detective to check on Perkins's ancestry. Even after discovering that she qualified for membership, the members of the D.A.R. still feared that Perkins was an adopted child of Jewish origin because the investigator had found no record of her birth in Boston in the year 1882.

In a national broadcast of the Bridges case, J. Parnell Thomas said, "This strong censure was made by a large membership of the Judiciary Committee of the House of Representatives, and by this censure the official acts of the Secretary of Labor and her associates have at least been officially condemned." Not once did he refer to the committee's unanimous opinion that there were no grounds for impeachment.

Although this was a lie, Perkins never fully recovered her good name, nor did she speak much of the incident. She merely said that "it hurt." In 1945 it was proven that Harry Bridges was neither a Communist nor subject to deportation. In 1948, J. Parnell Thomas's secretary accused him of listing people on his payroll who did not actually work for him and who "kicked back" their salaries to him.

Thomas was sentenced to six to eighteen months in prison and fined $10,000.

The impeachment fiasco strengthened Perkins's Christian faith. For years, she preferred the Anglo-Catholic or high Episcopal services. She confessed regularly and called her priest Father. Though Father Alfred Q. Plank conducted a Protestant service, he interwove Catholic rituals into the service. Perkins discussed her job experiences and family problems with Father Plank.

Since 1933, Perkins had gone once a month on a retreat to an Episcopal convent in Catonsville, Maryland. She usually spent a day or half a day there. Only Perkins's secretary Frances Jurkowitz knew where she went. The reverend mother and fourteen other nuns knew that she

All Saints' Convent of Catonsville, Maryland. (©Raf Seibert)

was the secretary of labor, but they did not tell anyone else. Except for two hours a day, the nuns observed the rule of silence. Perkins spent much of her time in prayer.

Perkins's concern over the protection of individual rights led her into an ongoing argument with J. Edgar Hoover, director of the FBI, over the fingerprinting of immigrants. She argued that privacy is the basis of liberty, and fingerprinting was a step toward destroying this precious democratic right. Roosevelt, however, insisted that all Americans voluntarily submit to fingerprinting.

By the end of 1939, much of the world was at war. In Europe, Adolph Hitler's armies bullied Austria and Czechoslovakia into submission without firing a shot. Then, on September 1, 1939, German troops invaded Poland, and World War II began. The United States remained neutral but was clearly on the side of Great Britain and the other allies opposed to Germany.

In May 1940, President Roosevelt decided that, because of growing problems with spies and saboteurs, the Immigration and Naturalization Service would be transferred from the Labor Department to the Department of Justice. The public interpreted the change as punishment for Perkins. This could not have come at a politically worse time for Perkins. Roosevelt had to know it would embarrass her. He could not bring himself to tell her about it and asked his wife Eleanor to do it for him. The U.S. Employment Service was transferred from the Department of Labor to the Federal Security Agency, and Perkins was cut out of the administration of the social security program.

The press quickly seized on what it interpreted as a decline in Perkins's influence. *Time* magazine reported that "of all the game in the Roosevelt preserve, Secretary of Labor Perkins has been most frequently chased, most savagely harried." But Perkins took the situation in stride. She resubmitted her resignation that year, but Roosevelt again refused to let her leave office.

The ongoing attacks might have dampened Perkins's popularity, but the more she was ridiculed, the more her admirers spoke out in her defense. In their memoirs, many cabinet members commented favorably about Perkins. Cordell Hull, secretary of state under Roosevelt from 1933 to 1944, wrote, "Miss Frances Perkins, Secretary of Labor, has never received the full credit she deserves for her ability and public services. She was unusually able, very practical, and brought vision and untiring energy to her work." James Farley, postmaster general and democratic chairman under Roosevelt, stated that Perkins was "a misunderstood and underappreciated woman, who had made no little contribution herself, even if one were to count nothing but the blows she took for others."

That year, Roosevelt became the first president to run for a third term. Perkins did not initially approve of Roosevelt running for a third term, but after the war in Europe began, she concluded that no one else had Roosevelt's ability in a crisis. Also, she was convinced the major work of the New Deal could only be completed by Roosevelt.

During the campaign, Roosevelt's Republican opponent, Wendell Willkie, said in a speech that if he won he would appoint a new secretary of labor, and it would "not be a woman." Roosevelt told Perkins that Willkie had insulted every woman in the United States by that statement and that it would cost him votes. He was right. In November, Roosevelt easily won reelection.

Perkins had planned to resign as secretary of labor, but Roosevelt again refused to accept her resignation. "I know who you are, what you are, what you'll do, what you won't do. You know me. You see lots of things that most people don't see. You keep me guarded against a lot of things that no new man walking in here would protect me from," he said. Roosevelt simply needed her loyalty.

NINE

World War II

Roosevelt declared a national emergency on May 27, 1941. Although the U.S. was officially neutral, Roosevelt presented a Selective Service Act to Congress. It was the first time a president had asked for a peace-time draft. War came to the United States suddenly when, on December 7, 1941, hundreds of Japanese planes attacked Pearl Harbor, the U.S. naval base in Hawaii. In the sneak attack the Japanese pilots sank or disabled nineteen U.S. ships, including six battleships, destroyed 150 planes, and killed 2,500 American soldiers, sailors, and civilians.

In her book, *The Roosevelt I Knew*, Perkins wrote:

The strangest cabinet meeting I attended was the one held at eight-thirty in the evening in the President's upstairs study in the White House on December 7, 1941. Most members of the cabinet had been out of town. They had been traced by the White House telephone operators and summoned hastily . . . I myself had been locked in a room in my club in New York (the Cosmopolitan Club) with my secretary, writing an important report. . . .

The President nodded as we came in, and in a low voice, began, "You all know what's happened. The attack began at one o'clock . . ." Francis Biddle, Attorney General, spoke, "Mr. President, several of us just arrived by plane. We don't know anything except a scare headline, 'Japanese Attack Pearl Harbor.' "

The U.S.S. Nevada *and the destroyers* Cassin *and* Downes *burn in the Pearl Harbor Navy Yard. The U.S.S.* Oglala, *in the foreground, has capsized.* (Courtesy of the Granger Collection.)

The president asked Frank Knox, secretary of the navy, to report on what had happened. Knox recounted the attack with interpolations by Secretary of War Stimson, Secretary of State Hull, and the president. It was agreed that Congress would be asked to declare war on Japan.

The new war would make tremendous demands on American labor. Even before the events at Pearl Harbor, Perkins suggested the creation of a board of mediation to help the defense industries settle disputes. In 1938, the Congress of Industrial Organizations (CIO) split from the AFL. Now there were two competing national labor organizations. Perkins met with their leaders and convinced them to accept the idea of a board of mediation and on March 19, 1941, Roosevelt created a National Defense Mediation Board, but it only lasted until November because of conflict between the two unions.

On December 18, 1941, eleven days after Pearl Harbor, twelve leaders from the AFL and CIO attended another five-day conference. This time they worked days and nights to the point of exhaustion. Finally the participants agreed to a moratorium on strikes and lockouts until the war ended. On January 12, 1942, Roosevelt established the national War Labor Board, which Perkins judged an imperfect success.

More than twenty million people died during World War II on the battlefields, in concentration camps, and in bombing raids on cities and towns, and another thirty million were wounded. The financial cost, plus property damage, remains impossible to calculate.

As men left their jobs to fight the war, employers hired women to build ships, planes, guns, trucks, and other supplies. In 1942, Perkins reported that at least four million U.S. women were working in war industries, and millions more in defense-related jobs. Prejudices against women workers as well as older and married workers relaxed during the war. Black women gained footholds in a number of occupational fields formerly closed to them, as did handicapped citizens.

Perkins coined the term "Rosie the Riveter" to describe the women who worked in war industries. Rosie the Riveter became an archetypal national heroine. The image of

A teacher before the war, Grace Weaver paints the American insignia on airplane wings. Like iconic Rosie, she contributes her labor to the American war effort. (Library of Congress)

When J. Howard Miller produced this poster in 1942, the female factory worker had no name. She became known as Rosie the Riveter, influenced by a 1943 Norman Rockwell painting that featured a brawny female riveter holding a lunch box labeled "Rosie." (Library of Congress.)

Rosie showed a white woman with a red bandanna with white polka dots wrapped around her short black hair. She is stripping her sleeve to show her muscle. Women laborers helped produce everything from an odd-looking little car named the Jeep to giant bombers such as the B-24. By 1942 military production in the U.S. equaled that of the combined power of Germany, Italy, and Japan, known as the Axis powers. Just before the attack on Pearl Harbor, 4,000 women worked in the manufacture of airplanes. One year later the figure skyrocketed to 200,000.

The Labor Department was accused of hurting war production when it objected to individuals working more than a ten-hour day, seven days a week. Perkins personally examined production curves and accident and absentee rates to support her dissenting position. She noted that fatigue led to accidents and shoddy work. She pointed out the lessons learned during WWI on the cumulative fatigue from being overworked. She used statistics to illustrate that safe working conditions and an eight-hour day would reduce costly industrial accidents and maximize efficiency. Roosevelt agreed. Only in mid-1943, after the pool of the unemployed had been drained, was the basic work week raised to forty-eight hours.

Perkins sat in on so many committees she complained that the Department of Labor had become a service agency for the military. Perkins became a member of virtually every interdepartmental committee in wartime Washington. She mastered the art of mediation, getting people to work together toward a common goal.

The war years were a time of great creativity for the United States. For the first time since the beginning of the Great Depression there were more jobs than there were workers to fill them. No longer was there a fear of unemployment. The output of steel and aluminum increased dramatically. The loss of natural rubber from Malaysia and Indonesia gave birth to a synthetic rubber industry. Radar sets were produced by radio manufacturers; airplane production went from one thousand to 50,000 airplanes a year.

The Labor Department worked to maintain what became known as the Home Front. The War Labor Board settled wage disputes by making decisions on a table of statistics called the Cost of Living Index. When labor leaders claimed the index was rigged to hold down wage increases, a technical analysis backed up the numbers.

As the war effort drained resources, the government started rationing essential items such as food, gas, and other scarce commodities. Rationing also kept prices from soaring out of control because of hoarding and profiteering. Coupons were handed out to the public for gas, meat, butter, sugar, and other foodstuffs. Babies received the same number of stamps as adults. The extra coupons helped large families, but smaller families especially felt the pinch.

During the war, birthday and holiday gifts were often war bonds sold to finance the war. Children in school saved their dimes for defense stamps they pasted in a book until they had enough to trade for a war bond. It was easier to buy bonds as presents because there was often little else to buy in the stores.

In the evening, families hovered around their radios for news of the war or to listen to one of Roosevelt's "fireside

Hundreds of posters created between 1941 and 1945 instructed citizens on contributing to the war effort at home. Most asked the public to buy war bonds, grow their own vegetables, or ration supplies such as rubber, gas, and food. (Library of Congress)

Roosevelt gave a series of thirty fireside chats between 1933 and 1944. They were broadcast directly from the White House to the radios in almost every American home. The chats gave people a sense of hope and security during the Great Depression and World War II. (Courtesy of the Granger Collection.)

chats." Pedestrians slowed their steps when they passed by homes with gold stars in the window, a sign indicating the loss of a soldier from that family.

In some ways it was an exhilarating time after the drudgery of the long depression. But it was also a wary period as the war dragged on and civilians waited for news from their loved ones fighting in Europe or in Asia and the Pacific Ocean.

In 1944, Roosevelt sought a fourth term as president. As a war-time president, he insisted that this was not the time for the country to change leaders. Perkins had seen him less often and for shorter periods during the war years. His focus was on foreign and military affairs. She noticed that he was visibly, and quickly, aging, but Roosevelt's health seemed sound enough to last through another term. He had always been such a vital, energetic man.

In reality, his health was poor. His physician never let anyone know how ill he was. He had a weak heart and was subject to fainting fits. His hands trembled, and his slack jaw indicated that he may have suffered minor strokes. He smoked heavily in an era when the damage caused by tobacco was not yet fully understood. Despite his health problems, Roosevelt was not ready to leave office.

Perkins had no official role at the Democratic convention, but she worked hard behind the scenes to keep the party from endorsing an Equal Rights Amendment (ERA) to the constitution. The National Women's Party had first proposed the ERA, which stated explicitly that women have the same rights as men under the U.S. Constitution, in 1923. It divided women's groups from the beginning. Social reformer Florence Kelley reluctantly turned against it because she thought it threatened a woman's legal protection for such things as maternity aid, mothers' pensions, and working conditions. She made opposition to the amendment a part of the Consumers League work. Mary Anderson of the Women's Bureau in the Department of Labor also opposed the amendment, as did the League of Women Voters. Perkins agreed with them, on the principle that it could allow the courts to deny women special protection.

When the convention opened, Perkins spoke against the amendment.

In October 1944, Perkins attended the funeral service for her old mentor, former New York Governor Al Smith. Eleanor Roosevelt represented the president at the services held in St. Patrick's Cathedral in New York City. Perkins remained loyal to Al Smith as she worked with Roosevelt. Smith had elevated her to positions higher than any attained by a woman when he was governor. Without Smith's help she would likely never have become secretary of labor and been able to do the things she did to help working people.

Roosevelt and Smith had drifted apart as Roosevelt attained national prominence. Smith wanted to be president, and it embittered him that someone he considered to be a child of privilege won the job he coveted. Perkins found Roosevelt more difficult to work with than Smith, who was usually quicker to understand the gist of a problem. To plant an idea in Roosevelt's mind, she had to explain it three times, but she could relay problems to Smith on the phone and he would understand. With Roosevelt she had to talk them over face to face and provide him with vivid examples. She tried to arrange longer conferences with Roosevelt for at least an hour every week. However, Roosevelt had a superior gift for seeing the overall picture presented by any situation and determining what had to be done on numerous fronts at the same time.

The following month, November, 1944, Franklin D. Roosevelt won his fourth term of office. Although little was said about Roosevelt's health, Perkins became concerned at a cabinet meeting the day before his fourth inauguration in January 1945. The president looked gray and his lips were blue. The newspaper pictures from his last inauguration revealed to the public a gaunt, sickly old man, much changed from the confidence-inspiring leader of 1933.

Two and a half months later, on April 12, 1945, President Roosevelt died in Warm Springs, Georgia, where he went to relax and treat his polio.

Perkins never lost her affection or admiration for Roosevelt. He had assured her the day before he left for Warm Springs that the war would end by May.

TEN

Lasting Legacy

After Roosevelt's death, Vice President Harry S. Truman assumed the role of president. Perkins offered Truman her resignation but he asked her to stay on until July 1, 1945. Perkins, a pioneer in labor reform, served an extraordinary twelve years as secretary of labor. Of the original New Deal cabinet of 1933, only Harold Ickes, secretary of the interior, put in more time than Perkins.

Perkins was determined to welcome the new secretary of labor, Lewis B. Schwellenbach, in a better manner than she had been in 1933. The offices then had been filthy with cockroaches, and she had to see that Hoover's labor secretary's papers and belongings were packed and delivered to his home. However, Schwellenbach seemed more embarrassed to succeed a woman than grateful for the way Perkins prepared for his transition.

Frances Perkins holds a piece of twine as she packs up her office at the Department of Labor after twelve years in Roosevelt's cabinet. A box of letters from three presidents sits by her chair. (Courtesy of Getty Images.)

On June 27, 1945, a dinner was held in Perkins's honor. Eighteen hundred people attended. Department of Labor employees chipped in to purchase several parting gifts—a typewriter, luggage, and a war bond.

At the testimonial dinner a host of labor, government, and industrial leaders spoke in her honor. Her old friend, Senator Robert Wagner, said, "Frances Perkins was, and still is, the supreme student of social conditions and remedial social legislation. She uncovered the facts, and told us what to do about them."

Truman agreed to send Perkins as a government representative to the International Labor Organization in Paris. Beyond that, her break with the Department of Labor was complete. She spent the summer in Maine with Susanna, who had divorced David Hare in 1943. They planned a visit to the Fallonsby Inn in North Sutton, New Hampshire, where her husband Paul was residing that summer.

Susanna was now twenty-nine. Perkins believed that she and her ex-husband had led a wayward life in Santa Fe, which had not provided Susanna with enough stability. Always aware of her husband Paul's problems, Perkins was fearful that her daughter might have inherited a tendency to emotional instability. Now Susanna had a chance to reconstruct her life.

Perkins found an apartment for Susanna in New York. Miranda Masocco, one of Susanna's friends from Santa Fe, moved in with her. One day Perkins sent instructions from Washington, D.C. on how Susanna and Miranda should dress for a reception for Princess Juliana of Holland. Miranda wore a simple black dress and pearls as requested, but Susanna appeared in a watermelon skirt with a green top and Capezio shoes tied up to the knees. She piled her hair on top of her head with a huge red rose and wore another red rose on a black velvet ribbon around her neck. Perkins was angry, and the two exchanged hot words. It was clear to most observers that mother and daughter had different personalities. Perkins believed in conformity and practicality; Susanna approached life more emotionally.

Susanna was eventually able to work through her divorce. By 1948, she had a job at the Metropolitan Museum of Art and she developed a life and identity for herself. In 1953, she married Calvert Coggeshall, an artist. The following year they had a son, Tomlin. Perkins was delighted to be a grandmother and lavished affection on her grandson.

Within weeks of Roosevelt's death, a literary agent, George Bye, suggested that Perkins write a biography of Roosevelt. Perkins hired several typists and a research assistant and began to write. She also bought a recording machine and narrated her memories. She was a better orator than a writer. Eventually she had piles of typed sheets, but little organization. Bye recommended she hire an editor, Howard Taubman, who arrived in Washington in late April and stayed for three weeks.

Taubman worked to rewrite and find a book in the pile of manuscript pages. Despite the hasty collaboration, *The Roosevelt I Knew* was a popular biography. It provided Perkins with financial security, which she had not had since 1918.

Perkins was not yet ready for full retirement, however. When President Truman asked what post she would like in his administration, Perkins suggested a position on the Social Security Board. When no position on the board came open, Truman appointed her to the three-member

Civil Service Commission, which supervised the federal work force. She worked there until 1953.

In her first speech at the Civil Service Commission, Perkins wasted no time dishing out her brazen opinions. She told an audience of government personnel workers that if she were asked to fill out some of the medical questions on a civil service application, she would write, "None of your business." She had no confidence in the government's ability, or desire, to keep personal information confidential.

Perkins also objected to investigators "snooping" on federal officeholders and job applicants. "What difference does it make to us if a man entertains ladies in his room?" asked the once-puritanical former cabinet member. "How is that going to affect on his ability to do his job?" She attacked government jargon, such as the use of the word "underprivileged" for the poor.

During the Korean War she complained that agencies employed only young, good-looking, and good-natured stenographers. She claimed that the two best stenographers in her own department were "grouchy, middle-aged frumps."

Perkins remained active in politics and in 1948 wrote a letter asking Eleanor Roosevelt to endorse Harry Truman for the presidency. Although Eleanor referred to Truman as a "weak and vacillating person, who made such poor appointments in his Cabinet," she eventually endorsed him for the Democratic Party's sake.

In 1951, while Perkins was still working at the Civil Service Commission, her husband, Paul, came to live with her again. He was seventy-five. She wrote Susanna that her father was not confused but showed little interest in anything, even reading. He remained dependent on her until his death on December 31, 1952. Perkins buried him in Maine in the family plot in the Glidden Cemetery.

When General Dwight D. Eisenhower, a Republican, became president in 1953, Perkins resigned from the Civil Service Commission. In her resignation speech in 1953, she admitted her work there had not always been stimulating, but that it had been a relief not to be always dealing with crises and problems, as she had in the Labor Department.

Although she was seventy-three, Perkins still did not want to retire. She accepted an invitation to lecture at the University of Illinois, where she held twelve seminar meetings about the Labor Department and the labor movement during the New Deal. She also gave university lectures on Roosevelt. Her talent as a lecturer won her several return appearances. More engagements followed, and suddenly she had a new career.

Perkins wanted to move back to New York to be closer to Susanna, her grandchild, her friends, and her old Mount Holyoke classmates. The School of Industrial and Labor Relations at Cornell University in Ithaca, New York, asked her to join as a visiting professor.

In New York she rented a room. As usual, Perkins needed little in the way of space, comfort, and familiar possessions. In addition to her work at Cornell, she agreed to lecture in Salzburg, Austria, and Bologna, Italy. In December

In her mid-seventies Perkins began a new career as a lecturer. Here she speaks at a Washington, D.C., event honoring the 25th Anniversary of the Social Security Act. (Courtesy of Mount Holyoke Archives and Special Collections.)

1957, she gave a university lecture on Al Smith, complete with mimicry of his accent. She described his clothes and gestures and spoke of his development from a boy in the Fulton Fish Market to a national leader, giving an inspiring example of what a young man can do for himself and for others. When she mentioned the event to her friend Agnes Leach, Perkins said, "It really was a standing ovation, for I asked the man next to me." She admitted that she could not see the back rows of the hall.

In the spring of 1960, Perkins received an invitation from the members of the Telluride Association at Cornell, composed of twenty-seven college and graduate students considered to be the intellectual elite of the university, to be a guest in residence in their house on the campus. No woman had ever lived in the house before. She accepted the honorable offer.

At Cornell, Perkins had no housekeeping duties. She had a house in which to give parties, and she thrived on the intellectual stimulation. Not since she shared a house in Washington with Mary Rumsey had she been happier. She was able to do great things for Telluride students, such as persuading Jim Farley and Henry Wallace to come to Cornell for seminars. She resurrected the Telluride House flower garden, gave the students Maine lobster dinners, and taught them how to throw sherry parties.

On March 25, 1961, Perkins helped to commemorate an event that had shaped her life fifty years earlier: the Triangle Shirtwaist Factory fire. She attended a memorial service held at the corner of Washington Place and Greene Street across the street from New York University with twelve elderly survivors of the fire to place a plaque on the building.

Perkins did have one disappointment during her last years. As part of her agreement with Cornell, she planned to write a biography of Al Smith similar to the one she had written on Roosevelt. She believed that much of Roosevelt's New Deal legislation, particularly the industrial and labor legislation, had its origins in Smith's years as speaker of the assembly and as governor of New York. Roosevelt had not been a member of the New York State Factory Investigating Commission and had not been active in social and industrial reform early in his career. Perkins was eager to help Smith get credit she thought he was due. But she could not finish the book alone and again sought the help of Howard Taubman, who was too busy. She later asked Daniel Patrick Moynihan, who was then assistant secretary of labor, but his work became too pressing.

Soon after, her health declined. In the spring of 1965, Perkins went to Washington, saw old friends, and went on retreat at All Saints' Convent. Back in New York, she attended the ballet with an old friend. The next day Perkins suffered several strokes and died on May 14, 1965, at the age of eighty-five.

Perkins was buried next to her husband. Susanna placed a simple stone on her mother's grave that read: Frances Perkins Wilson 1880-1965 Secretary of Labor of USA 1933-1945.

After Perkins's death, the material for the Al Smith book she so wanted to write was used by Matthew and Hannah Josephson in their work, *Al Smith: Hero of the Cities, A Political Portrait Drawing Upon the Papers of Frances Perkins*.

When news of Perkins' death reached Washington, Secretary of Labor W. Willard Wirtz paid his predecessor a most fitting tribute: "Every man and woman in America who works at a living wage, under safe conditions, for reasonable hours, or who is protected by unemployment insurance or Social Security is Frances Perkins' debtor."

The Perkins Program was instituted at Mount Holyoke, offering a scholarship for women twenty-four and above, as well as a graduate fellowship. In 1986, Marjory and Robert

Jo Polseno portrays Perkins standing guard over a mill town. The image came with U.S. postage stamps commemorating Perkins's legacy. The stamp was released on April 10, 1980, one hundred years from Frances Perkins's birth.

Potts made a documentary film about Perkins titled *You May Call Her Madam* about the life of Frances Perkins.

In 1980, Congress named the new Washington, D.C. headquarters of the Labor Department in honor of Perkins. This was the first time a federal government building bore a woman's name. That year, the U.S. Postal Service issued a fifteen-cent stamp bearing an image of Perkins wearing the small black tricorn hat that had become her trademark during her years as a cabinet officer. In 1982, Perkins was posthumously inducted into the National Women's Hall of Fame and in 1988 into the Labor Hall of Fame.

Perkins liked to challenge young people to ask themselves: "What is my duty?" She would tell students,

President Jimmy Carter gives an address at the dedication of the Frances Perkins Department of Labor Building in April of 1980. (Department of Labor)

"There is always a large horizon . . .There is much to be done . . .I am not going to be doing it! It is up to you to contribute some small part to a program of human betterment for all time."

Perkins knew that the fight to maintain labor standards would never end. Factories are still in need of regular inspection. Advances had been made to see that everyone has access to medical care, but inadequate health care, systemic poverty, and unemployment remain great concerns in the United States. Perkins knew the job would never be completed, but she had faith that another generation of people who believed in social justice would fight to make life better for all Americans.

It took twenty years before another president, Dwight Eisenhower, appointed a woman, Oveta Culp Hobby, in 1953, to the newly created cabinet position as Secretary of Health, Education and Welfare. Forty-two years passed before President Gerald Ford appointed Carla Hills as Secretary of Housing and Urban Development in 1975. Since then, women have been appointed to several cabinet-level positions and have been elected to the Senate and House of Representatives. Women have also been elected as governors of several states. A woman has not yet been elected president of the United States, but that will likely change someday. When it does, she will owe her election, at least in part, to the hard work and dedication of Frances Perkins, the first woman to serve in a president's cabinet.

TIMELINE

1880	Fanny Coralie Perkins born on April 10 in Boston, Massachusetts.
1902	Graduates from Mount Holyoke College with a degree in chemistry and physics.
1904-1907	Teaches physics and biology in Lake Forest, Illinois. Volunteers at Hull House and Chicago Commons. Leaves teaching for social work.
1908	General secretary of the Philadelphia Research and Protective Association. Studies economics and sociology at the University of Pennsylvania. Does social casework. Earns a graduate fellowship at Columbia University in New York.
1910	Receives a master's degree in political science on June 10. Becomes Executive Secretary, National Consumers League. Begins investigative work of working conditions in 100 bakeries and of fires in factories. Fights for protective legislation, especially for women and children.
1911	Witnesses Triangle Shirtwaist Factory Fire in which 146 workers, mostly girls and young women, died.

Helps Factory Investigating Commission document poor working conditions in New York. Serves as expert witness. Lobbies to pass a 54-hour bill for working women.

1912   Becomes executive secretary for the Committee on Public Safety.

1913   Marries Paul C. Wilson.

1916   Daughter Susanna is born.

1917   World War I. Perkins becomes executive director of the New York Council of Organizations for War Service. Organizes and runs the Maternity Center Association.

1918   Paul Wilson becomes a chronic invalid. Women win the right to vote in New York.

1919   Perkins appointed to the New York State Industrial Commission by Governor Al Smith.

1920   All women gain suffrage by passage of the 19th Amendment.

1921   Serves as executive secretary for the Council on Immigrant Education.

1922   Reappointed as a member of the New York State Industrial Commission.

1926   Becomes chairman of the Industrial Board of New York State Labor Department.

1929   Appointed New York State industrial commissioner by Governor Franklin D. Roosevelt.

1933   Appointed U.S. secretary of labor by President Franklin D. Roosevelt—first woman cabinet officer in U.S. history. Helps initiate Civilian Conservation Corps (CCC), Works Progress Administration (WPA), and Federal-State Unemployment Insurance System.

1934   Helps bring the U.S. into the International Labor Organization (ILO); writes *People at Work*.

1935	Helps initiate Social Security System.
1938	Helps to pass the Fair Labor Standards Act (FLSA) including minimum wage, overtime pay, and child labor regulation.
1939	Defends herself against an impeachment resolution.
1941	The U.S. battles in World War II through 1945. Serves as mediator on committees and disentangles many labor problems.
1945	Death of Franklin D. Roosevelt. Perkins offers President Harry S. Truman her resignation.
1945-1946	Writes *The Roosevelt I Knew*. Truman appoints her to U.S. Civil Service Commission.
1952	Paul Wilson dies.
1953	Resigns from Civil Service Commission.
1957-1966	Becomes a lecturer and visiting professor, then resident professor at Cornell University.
1965	Dies on May 14 in New York City.
1980	Dedication of the U.S. Department of Labor Francis Perkins Building, the Department of Labor's headquarters in Washington, D.C.; The United States Postal Service releases a Frances Perkins commemorative stamp on April 10.

SOURCES

CHAPTER ONE: Happy Days

p. 12, "I've been thinking . . . political consideration."
Frances Perkins, *The Roosevelt I Knew* (New York:
Harper & Row, 1946), 151-2.

p. 15, "If you have anything . . ." Frances Perkins, "Eight Years
as Madame Secretary," *Fortune*, 24 (Sept. 1941), 8.

p. 17, "loquacious linguist," Don Lawson, *Frances Perkins:
First Lady of the Cabinet* (New York: Abelard-Schuman,
1966), 24.

p. 17, "wretched physics laboratory" George Martin, *Madam
Secretary, Frances Perkins* (Boston: Houghton Mifflin
Company, 1976), 47.

p. 17, "the girl who had . . ." Lillian Holmen Mohr, *Frances
Perkins, That Woman in FDR's Cabinet!* (Croton-on-Hudson,
NY: North River Press, 1979), 17.

CHAPTER TWO: The Pursuit of Social Justice

p. 24, "the pursuit of social . . ." Perkins, *The Roosevelt*, 10.

p. 24, ". . . he had been the first . . ." Perkins's Oral History
at Columbia University, Book 1, 187-188, 211-214.

p. 24, "Out of the period that . . ." Penny Colman, *A Woman Unafraid: The Achievements of Frances Perkins* (New York: Atheneum, 1993), 14.

p. 26, "half-way to the . . ." Martin, *Madam Secretary*, 57.

p. 28, "Sam Smith!" Ibid., 67.

p. 29, "From the admiration . . . early twenties." George N. Caylor, "Perkins 1882-1963 (sic), A Memoir," New York Public Library, New York, July 4-5, 1965, 8.

p. 30, "A child of the poor . . ." Martin, *Madam Secretary*, 73.

p. 32, "peculiar style of . . ." Mohr, *Frances Perkins, That Woman,* 41.

p. 32, "at the top of his lungs" Ibid., 42.

p. 35, ". . . a fine, bright . . ." Leon Stein, *The Triangle Fire* (Philadelphia & New York: J. B. Lippincott Company, 1962), 211-12.

p. 36, "out of that terrible . . ." Ibid.

CHAPTER THREE: Fiery Young Idealist

p. 40, "I took it hard . . ." Perkins, *The Roosevelt I Knew*, 14.

p. 42-43, "I feel you and . . ." Letter Paul C. Wilson to Perkins, September 8, 1913, and Perkins to Paul C. Wilson, September 9, 1913, Perkins Papers, Coggeshall.

p. 44, "shack in the country" Mohr, *Frances Perkins, That Woman*, 179.

p. 44, "Oh, Frances, why did . . ." Martin, *Madam Secretary*, 125.

p. 46, ". . . the most successful piece . . ." Ibid., 133.

p. 48-49, "How would you like . . . rely on it" Ibid., 142.

p. 49, "Glory be . . ." Ibid., 143.

p. 52, "Kiss my ass..." Ibid., 155.

p. 54, "You sure had your nerve . . ." Matthew and Hannah Josephson, *Al Smith: Hero of the Cities* (Boston:

Houghton Mifflin Company, 1969), 230.

p. 55, "I have met . . ." *Manchester Guardian*, January 1928, Mount Holyoke alumnae file.

p. 56, "I stepped out . . ." Colman, *A Woman Unafraid*, 45.

CHAPTER FOUR: A Responsible Public Officer

p. 65, "Sooner or later . . ." Lawson, *Frances Perkins: First Lady,* 54.

p. 70, "Apologize! . . . good work!" Ibid., 60.

p. 70, "We're not just dealing with . . ." Ibid., 61.

CHAPTER FIVE: The Struggle for National Recovery

p. 73-74, "What do you regard . . . its source." Alice R. Hager, "Miss Perkins Talks of the Tasks Ahead," *New York Times Magazine*, May 7, 1933, 3, 17.

p. 78, "The overwhelming argument . . ." Colman, *A Woman Unafraid*, 60.

p. 78, "Labor can never..." Martin, *Madam Secretary*, 3.

CHAPTER SIX: Making the New Deal Work

p. 82, "Madam Secretary" Mohr, *Frances Perkins, That Woman*, 128.

p. 89, ". . . there was a great . . ." Perkins, *The Roosevelt*, 210.

p. 91, "I call it serious . . ." Martin, *Madam Secretary*, 320.

p. 92, "There have been . . ." Colman, *A Woman Unafraid*, 79.

CHAPTER SEVEN: Social Security

p. 97, "You care about . . ." Perkins, *The Roosevelt*, 281.

p. 99, As I see it . . ." Arthur M. Schlesinger, Jr., *The Coming of the New Deal: The Age of Roosevelt* (Boston: Houghton Mifflin Company, 1958), 304.

p.103, "It represented the thinking of . . ." Mohr, *Frances Perkins, That Woman*, 212.

p. 104, "This third anniversary . . ." Bill Severn, *Frances Perkins: A Member of the Cabinet* (New York: Hawthorne Books, Inc., 1976), 187.

p. 105, "I have an idea . . ." Mohr, *Frances Perkins, That Woman*, 213.

CHAPTER EIGHT: Politics and Honor

p. 110, ". . . a foreign-born Jew." Colman, *A Woman Unafraid*, 90.

p. 113, "woozy in the head." Mohr, *Frances Perkins, That Woman*, 278.

p. 116-117, ". . . to protect me . . ." Ibid., 256.

p. 117, "I realize that . . ." Joseph P. Lash, *Eleanor and Franklin* (New York: W. W. Norton and Company, 1971), 463-464.

p. 117, "Frances Wadski Perkins" Martin, *Madam Secretary*, 418.

p. 118, "If I were a Jew . . ." Colman, *A Woman Unafraid*, 91.

p. 118, "This strong censure . . ." *Congressional Record*, Additional Views, March 30, 1939, p. 13552.

p. 118, "it hurt." Mohr, *Frances Perkins, That Woman*, 260.

p. 121, "of all the game . . ." *Time*, April 28, 1941, 18.

p. 121, "Miss Frances Perkins . . ." Cordell Hull, *The Memoirs of Cordell Hull* (New York: The Macmillan Company, 1948), I, 210.

p. 121, ". . . a misunderstood . . ." James A. Farley, *Jim Farley's Story: The Roosevelt Years* (New York: McGraw-Hill Book Company, 1948), 328.

p. 122, ". . . not be a woman." Perkins, *The Roosevelt*, 117.

p. 122, "I know who . . ." Colman, *A Woman Unafraid*, 95.

CHAPTER NINE: World War II

p. 123-124, "The strangest cabinet . . ." Perkins, *The Roosevelt*, 377-379.

CHAPTER TEN: Lasting Legacy

p. 136, "Frances Perkins was . . ." "Testimonial Dinner," *Washington Evening Star*, June 27, 1945, June 28, 1945, Perkins Papers at Columbia.

p. 138, "None of your business" Martin, *Madam Secretary*, 477.

p. 138, "What difference does . . ." Mohr, *Frances Perkins, That Woman*, 284.

p. 138, "grouchy, middle-aged frumps." Ibid., 285.

p. 138, ". . . weak and vacillating . . ." Joseph Lash, *Eleanor: The Years Alone* (New York: New American Library, 1972), 152.

p. 140, "It really was . . ." Martin, *Madam Secretary*, 484.

p. 142, "Every man and woman . . ." Lawson, *Frances Perkins: First Lady*, 153.

p. 143-144, "What is my duty?" Perkins's Syracuse speech, February 12, 1960.

BIBLIOGRAPHY

Colman, Penny. *A Woman Unafraid: The Achievements of Frances Perkins*. New York: Atheneum, 1993.

Daniels, Doris Groshen. *Always a Sister: The Feminism of Lillian D. Wald*. New York: The Feminist Press at The City University of New York, 1989.

Farley, James A. *Jim Farley's Story: The Roosevelt Years*. New York: McGraw-Hill Book Company, Inc., 1948.

Goldmark, Josephine. *Impatient Crusader: Florence Kelley's Life Story*. Urbana: University of Illinois Press, 1953.

Hager, Alice R. "Miss Perkins Talks of the Tasks Ahead." *New York Times Magazine*, May 7, 1933: 3, 17.

Hull, Cordell, with Andrew Berding. *The Memoirs of Cordell Hull*. New York: The Macmillan Company, 1948.

Josephson, Matthew, and Hannah Josephson. *Al Smith: Hero of the Cities*. Boston: Houghton Mifflin Company, 1969.

Lash, Joseph P. *Eleanor and Franklin*. New York: W. W. Norton and Company, Inc., 1971.

———. *Eleanor: The Years Alone* New York: New American Library, 1972.

Lawson, Don. *Frances Perkins: First Lady of the Cabinet.*
New York: Abelard-Schuman, 1966.

Martin, George. *Madam Secretary, Frances Perkins.*
Boston: Houghton Mifflin Company, 1976.

Mohr, Lillian Holmen. *Frances Perkins, That Woman in
FDR's Cabinet!* Croton-on-Hudson, New York:
North River Press, 1979.

Perkins, Frances. "Eight Years as Madame Secretary."
Fortune. 24 (Sept. 1941): 76-79, 94.

──────. *The Roosevelt I Knew.* New York: Harper and Row,
1946.

Roosevelt, Eleanor. *This I Remember.* New York: Harper
and Brothers, 1949.

Roosevelt, Eleanor, and Lorena A. Hickok. *Ladies of
Courage.* New York: G. P. Putnam's Sons, 1954.

Severn, Bill. *Frances Perkins: A Member of the Cabinet.*
New York: Hawthorne Books, Inc., 1976.

Stein, Leon. *The Triangle Fire.* New York: J. B. Lippincott
Company, 1962.

Ward, Paul W. "Please Excuse Miss Perkins." *The Nation*,
March 27, 1935, vol. 140, 353.

WEB SITES

Department of Labor history
http://dol.gov/oasam/programs/history/perkins.htm

**Columbia University Libraries Oral History Research
Office: Notable New Yorkers**
http://www.columbia.edu/cu/lweb/digital/collections/nny/
perkinsf/index.html

Social Security Online
http://www.ssa.gov/history/fperkins.html

Spartacus Educational
http://www.spartacus.schoolnet.co.uk/USARperkins.htm

INDEX